What is Your Middle Credit Score?

Your Path to Financial Literacy & Empowerment

Glenn Clark

Printed in the United States of America

First Edition

ISBN: 979-8-9945570-0-6
     51999
     9 798994 557006

Publisher:
Middle Credit Score LLC
Gilbert, Arizona
MiddleCreditScore.com

middle credit score®

To every consumer who was never taught how credit really works and chose to learn anyway.

CONTENTS

SECTION I: FOUNDATIONS OF CREDIT
What credit is, how it works, and why it matters

Chapters in Section I:

CONTENTS

SECTION II: APPLYING CREDIT WITH INTENTION
Using credit strategically in real life

Chapters in Section II:

CONTENTS

CONTENTS

SECTION IV: REFERENCE & RESOURCES
Additional information about credit terms, the book, and the author

Section IV:

How to Use This Book (Read This First)

This is not a book you read once and put on a shelf.

I wrote this as a **working reference,** the kind you can come back to when life changes, when money gets tight, when a lender tells you "No," or when you're ready to level up and stop guessing. If you try to read it cover-to-cover like a novel, you *can*… but that's not the best way to use it.

You don't have to read it straight through

Some chapters will matter to you **right now**. Others won't matter until later when you're buying your first home, rebuilding after a setback, planning a refinance, starting a business, or preparing for retirement. That's normal.

Use it by life stage

Your credit and finances move in seasons. This book is designed so you can begin based on where you are today:

- **Starting out/rebuilding:** Get clarity fast, learn what affects your score, and stop the small mistakes that cost you big.
- **Preparing for homeownership:** Learn what lenders look for, how to strengthen your profile, and how to avoid last-minute surprises.

- **Family growth/career growth:** Understand how debt, utilization, and budgeting choices affect your future borrowing power.
- **Wealth-building mode:** Shift from "fixing credit" to **protecting credit** and using it strategically (without getting played by interest).
- **Major transitions:** Divorce, job change, medical bills, and late payments. This book helps you respond with a plan instead of panic.

Treat this as a reference, not a one-time read

Think of each chapter like a tool in a toolbox. You do not carry every tool in your hand; you reach for the right one when you need it.

Here's the best way to get results from this book:

1. **Skim first.** Read the headings, key points, and examples to understand what's inside.
2. **Pick one goal.** Don't try to fix everything at once. Choose the one outcome you want most:
   o Raise your score
   o Remove harmful errors
   o Pay down debt efficiently
   o Prepare for a mortgage
   o Avoid future score drops
3. **Take action in small steps.** A few correct moves, repeated consistently, beat "credit panic" every time.

4. Throughout this book, you'll find **_97 real-life client examples and solutions_** drawn directly from my work with consumers, families, and professionals over decades in lending, real estate, and credit strategy. These are not hypotheticals. They are the patterns, mistakes, corrections, and wins I've seen repeatedly in the real world. If a situation feels familiar, it's because it is.

Revisit chapters as your situation changes. Your next season will require a different strategy than your current one.

Pay special attention to the "From My Files" examples

Those examples are not theory; they're real-world situations pulled from the work I have done with consumers over the years. They
are there because most people do not need more motivation... they need **proof**, clarity, and a strategy that works in real life. When you see a client example that sounds like you, slow down. Read it twice. That is usually where the breakthroughs happen.

The promise of this book

If you use this book the right way, like a reference, your financial confidence will grow. You will stop feeling powerless when it comes to credit, lenders, and big decisions. You will understand what matters, what does not, and what to do next.

That is the point.

When you are ready, turn the page.

Introduction

Why Your Middle Credit Score® Matters More Than You've Been Told

For nearly three decades, I have sat across kitchen tables, conference desks, and closing rooms from people who were doing everything they believed was right, working hard, paying bills, raising families, yet still found themselves confused, frustrated, or shut out when it came time to buy a home, refinance, or take the next financial step. I have seen the disappointment in their eyes when they were told "your credit is not quite there," without anyone explaining what that really meant or how to fix it. That experience is the reason this book exists.

I have been in this industry long enough to see credit from every angle. I have been a top-producing loan officer, a former co-owner of a mortgage company, and now the owner and founder of **Browse Lenders®** and **Middle Credit Score®**. I have reviewed tens of thousands of credit reports line by line, not just glancing at a score, but understanding the story behind it, and what I've learned is this: most consumers are not failing credit; they were never properly taught how credit works.

One of the biggest misconceptions I see is the belief that "a credit score is a credit score." It isn't. **In most mortgage decisions, lenders do not use your highest or lowest credit score—they price loans using the middle score.** In real lending decisions, especially for mortgages, the Middle Credit Score® matters most. Not the highest score. Not the lowest. The middle score. And yet, very few people are ever told this, let alone taught how to protect it, improve it, or use it strategically. That knowledge gap costs people real money, higher interest rates, worse loan terms, delayed opportunities, and sometimes lost dreams.

This book was written to change that.

You do not need to become a credit expert. You do not need to memorize scoring formulas or obsess over every number. What you *do* need is clarity, clarity about how lenders think, how credit decisions are made, and how small, intentional habits compound into long-term financial power. That's what I aim to give you here.

Throughout this book, I'll walk you through credit the way I've explained it to my own clients, plain language, real examples, no fluff. You'll learn how the Middle Credit Score is calculated, why it matters at different stages of life, how to avoid common traps, and

how to build a system that protects your financial future. This isn't theory. These are strategies I've watched work repeatedly.

Whether your goal is homeownership, refinancing, investing, business ownership, or simply financial peace of mind, understanding your Middle Credit Score gives you leverage. It gives you control. And most importantly, it gives you options.

This book is not about perfection. It's about progress. It's about putting you back in the driver's seat of your financial life, fully equipped with the knowledge, habits, and confidence to move forward intentionally.

Let's begin.

Understanding Credit Scores

The Foundation of Financial Success

When it comes to building a secure financial future, understanding your credit score is non-negotiable. This three-digit number may look deceptively simple, but it controls what your money can do next. It shapes the cost of borrowing, the ease of renting, the terms you're offered, and the speed at which you can move through life's most significant milestones. Most people do not realize that the credit score is not just a rating, it is a pricing tool, and if you don't understand it, you'll still pay for it.

I have watched borrowers avoid credit because it feels intimidating. They do not check reports, they do not ask questions, and they do not challenge inaccuracies until the moment they want something big: a home, a car, a business loan, a clean restart. That is when the credit score stops being abstract and becomes immediate. It is also when people learn the hard way that credit is not about your worth. It is about your pattern. It is a mirror of behavior, not identity.

The good news is that credit scores are not fixed. They respond to decisions. With the proper knowledge, you can improve your score and regain control over what lenders, landlords, and insurers see. This chapter will strip away the mystery and replace it with clarity. By the end, you will know what a credit score measures, why it matters, how it is calculated, and why the Middle Credit Score becomes the deciding number for major lending decisions.

Section 1: Why Credit Scores Matter

Your Middle Credit Score® is a silent storyteller of your financial life. It follows you into rooms you have never been inside such as underwriting departments, leasing offices, insurance pricing models and speaks on your behalf before you ever get the chance. Whether you're applying for a mortgage, renting an apartment, negotiating a car loan, or even trying to reduce certain monthly costs, your score is often the first filter.

A strong score does not just help you qualify. It changes your leverage. It determines whether money is offered to you at a fair price or whether you're charged extra for the same opportunity.

This is where the real cost lives: not in whether you get approved, but in how much more you pay when you do.

I have seen borrowers do everything "right" in their day-to-day lives from having a steady job, consistent income, even savings and still get hit with higher rates because they never learned how credit is measured. Once they understand what the score rewards and punishes, their decisions become intentional. That shift is where financial power begins.

From My Client Files - Example 1 (Chapter 1):
Sarah and Michael's Mortgage Journey

Sarah and Michael were first-time homebuyers with similar incomes, similar savings, and the same goal: to buy in the same neighborhood. Sarah's score was strong because she kept balances low and never missed a payment. Michael's score was lower, not because he was reckless, but because he had a few late payments and ran high utilization for extended periods. When they applied, Sarah was offered better terms. Michael was offered higher pricing, and over the life of the loan, that difference became a six-figure penalty. Michael left the process with something most borrowers are never aware of. He finally understood that "paying on time" is not the whole story; how you use credit matters just as much.

Section 2: Introducing the Middle Credit Score®

When it comes to major lending decisions, not all credit scores are treated equally. Consumers often assume the highest score "wins." Lenders do not operate that way, especially in mortgage underwriting. When a lender pulls your credit, they typically see three scores: Experian, Equifax, and TransUnion. Instead of choosing the highest or averaging them, they rely on the Middle Credit Score, the median of the three.

The Middle Credit Score matters because it reduces risk. It protects the lender from being misled by an unusually high score and protects you from being unfairly penalized by one unusually low score caused by a reporting issue. It is the most balanced representation of your credit standing at that moment because it is the number lenders build pricing around, it becomes the number you should understand, monitor, and optimize.

From My Client Files - Example 2 (Chapter 1): Sarah's Middle Credit Score® and Homeownership

---

Annette assumed her strongest credit score would drive the loan decision. Like many borrowers, she believed the highest number would carry the most weight. What she did not realize was that her three bureau scores were not aligned because one was strong, one was weaker than expected, and the lender would price the loan based on the middle score, not the best one. That single realization changed how she approached the entire process. She stopped hoping the lender would "look past" the lower score and started focusing on what the lender would use.

Once her strategy matched reality, her actions became more precise. She paid down revolving balances to tighten utilization, corrected a reporting error that was dragging one bureau down, and avoided unnecessary inquiries that could introduce new risk. None of the moves were dramatic. There were no shortcuts. But each decision was intentional, and each one supported the score that mattered in the approval process.

The result was not a headline-worthy jump; it was a tier shift, and that is where real savings live. Better pricing, lower monthly payments, and thousands saved over the life of the loan came not from chasing the highest possible number, but from positioning the Middle Credit Score® correctly. Sarah did not just qualify for a mortgage; she qualified on terms that matched her true financial reliability.

Section 3: Why the Middle Credit Score Is Critical

The Middle Credit Score is the most equitable way to evaluate a borrower when credit reporting is not perfectly consistent. Because the three bureaus may contain different data, scores can vary. The middle score neutralizes extremes and gives underwriting a stable anchor point.

This is especially important because one bureau can carry an error that the others do not. A duplicate account, an outdated delinquency, or a misreported balance can drag a score down even if your overall credit behavior is improving. The Middle Credit Score can prevent one flawed report from dominating your outcome, but it does not replace the need to monitor and correct your reports.

From My Client Files - Example 3 (Chapter 1):
Finding Fairness Through the Middle Credit Score®

Maria did everything people are told to do when preparing for homeownership. She saved consistently, maintained steady employment, and lived within her means. On paper, she looked ready. But when her lender pulled her credit, one bureau still reflected an old delinquency that had already been resolved. Two bureaus told the correct story. One did not. And that single outdated item threatened to price her loan as if her entire financial profile were unstable.

This is where understanding the Middle Credit Score® mattered. Instead of being evaluated based on the worst version of her file, the lender relied on the middle score, the score that best represented her actual credit behavior across all three bureaus. That approach did not "give her a break." It gave her fairness. The loan terms she received aligned with who she really was as a borrower, not with an error that no longer reflected reality.

What stood out most was not just the outcome, it was what happened next. After closing, Maria did not move on and forget about her credit. She understood that credit is not something you fix once and ignore. She became proactive. She reviewed her reports regularly, verified that updates were reflected correctly, and corrected discrepancies before they became urgent. She stopped reacting to credit and started managing it.

Maria's story is a reminder of why the Middle Credit Score® exists. Credit is not about perfection; it is about accuracy and consistency. When the system evaluates you correctly, it rewards discipline. And when you understand how that evaluation works, you protect yourself from paying more than you should for the same opportunity.

Key Takeaways from Maria's Experience

1. *One outdated item on a single bureau can unfairly impact loan pricing.*
2. *The Middle Credit Score® often provides a more accurate reflection of true credit behavior.*

3. *Reviewing and correcting reports before applying, prevents unnecessary cost.*

4. *Credit fairness is achieved through understanding, not hope.*

Section 4: Building the Framework for Success

A credit score is not a mystery once you understand what it responds to. It responds to habits that include consistency, balance, patience, and timing. The people who win with credit are not always the people with the most money. They are the people who understand the rules and stop playing blind.

This framework begins with awareness and develops into routine. In practice, that means consistently reviewing your reports, knowing your Middle Credit Score, and managing credit as a tool rather than a threat. A defined framework creates stability and helps you avoid reactive decisions such as closing old accounts, opening new credit hastily, or allowing utilization to surge just before an application.

From My Client Files - Example 4 (Chapter 1): Building a Credit Framework for Success

---

Sabrina came in frustrated, not because she was reckless, but because she felt she was doing everything right and still was not seeing the results she expected. She paid her bills, avoided unnecessary debt, and believed her credit was "fine." But frustration often shows up when effort is not aligned with how the system measures risk. That disconnect is where many responsible borrowers get stuck.

When we reviewed her file, the issue became clear. One bureau was reporting inconsistently, and her revolving utilization was higher than she realized, enough to suppress her Middle Credit Score®, despite otherwise solid behavior. Once she understood the mechanics behind the number, the problem stopped feeling personal. It became technical. And technical problems can be fixed with structure.

Sabrina made small, focused changes instead of dramatic ones. She corrected the bureau discrepancy, strategically reduced utilization, and stayed consistent. Six months later, her middle score moved into a stronger tier, and she qualified for terms that finally matched her true financial reliability. But the biggest shift wasn't the score, it was her confidence. She stopped guessing and started deciding from knowledge, which is exactly how credit becomes a tool instead of a source of stress.

Section 5: What Is a Credit Score?

A credit score is a shorthand risk assessment. It tells a lender how you've handled borrowed money in the past and how likely you are to repay in the future. It's not a moral judgment. It's not a personality test. It's simply a pattern of behavior translated into a number.

A lender doesn't have time to read the story of your entire financial life. The score helps them decide quickly. A higher score typically signals lower risk, which translates into better pricing. A lower score signals higher risk, which is reflected in higher pricing. This is why understanding credit isn't optional because whether you know it or not, the pricing still applies.

From My Client Files - Example 5 (Chapter 1):
April's Journey to Financial Freedom

April was not irresponsible, she was uninformed. She worked steadily, paid most of her bills on time, and was not reckless with money, yet her credit score felt stuck and discouraging. Old missed payments from years earlier still lingered, and credit card balances from a difficult season kept dragging her score down. Every time she checked her credit, it felt less like information and more like judgment. No one had ever explained why her score behaved the way it did.

When we reviewed all three credit reports together, the picture became clear. Her utilization remained high even with on-time payments, accounts were reported inconsistently across bureaus, and payment timing worked against her without her realizing it. None of this meant she was bad with money, it meant the system was doing exactly what it was designed to do, and she had never been taught how to navigate it. We built a simple, disciplined plan focused on lowering utilization strategically, correcting reporting issues, and aligning her actions with how credit scoring works.

Her score improved, but that was not the real victory. The real change was confidence. April stopped fearing her credit reports and started using them as a guide. She understood what mattered, what did not, and how her daily decisions influenced outcomes. Credit stopped controlling her behavior, and she stopped avoiding it. That's when financial freedom truly began, not with a number, but with understanding.

Section 6: The Purpose of a Credit Score

The purpose of a credit score is standardization. It gives lenders, insurers, and landlords a common language for evaluating risk. That's why it can impact more than borrowing. In certain situations, it influences insurance pricing and housing approval. It can shape whether you are required to pay deposits, accept strict terms, or pay higher monthly costs.

This is why credit health is not just about getting approved. It is about keeping your life affordable. A stronger score reduces friction. It improves terms. It gives you options, and options are a form of financial freedom.

From My Client Files - Example 6 (Chapter 1): Tenant's Journey Through the Impact of a Credit Score

---

Maya had done what most responsible renters are told to do. She saved for her security deposit, stabilized her income, and believed she was finally ready to move forward. But when her rental application was denied, the reason caught her off guard: her credit score did not yet reflect the stability she had recently built. What Maya learned in that moment is something many people do not realize until it costs them an opportunity—credit history does not reset just because life improves.

Once she understood that credit is a record of past behavior, not present intentions, her approach shifted. She began monitoring her reports regularly, correcting outdated information, and staying consistent with payments and utilization. Over time, her score caught up to the person she had become. When it did, her options expanded. That is the real role of credit, not to judge who you are today, but to document who you've proven yourself to be over time.

Section 7: Key Components of a Credit Score

Credit scores are built from a handful of core components, and each one tells the system a different story. Payment history communicates reliability. Utilization communicates restraint. Length of history communicates stability. Mix communicates experience. Inquiries communicate timing and pressure.

Most people focus on the wrong thing: they chase points rather than manage behavior. When you stop obsessing over the number and start working on the components, the score follows. This chapter is not here to make you memorize percentages. It is here to teach you what moves the needle in the real world.

From My Client Files - Example 7 (Chapter 1): Stephanie's Business Loan Wake-Up Call

---

Stephanie did not experience a financial collapse; she experienced a misunderstanding of how credit risk is measured. During a slow business season, she leaned more heavily on revolving credit to keep operations moving and missed a couple of payment deadlines while juggling cash flow. From her perspective, she was surviving a temporary dip. From a lender's perspective, her rising utilization and recent late payments signaled instability. When she applied for financing, the response was immediate and frustrating: higher rates, tighter terms, and limited options.

Once we broke down her reports, the solution became clear and practical. We focused on restoring payment consistency, reducing utilization deliberately rather than emotionally, and aligning her behavior with what lenders evaluate. As her balances trended down and on-time payments stacked up, her score recovered, and so did her access to capital. Stephanie's experience is a reminder that the credit system is responsive. It penalizes neglect quickly, but it also rewards correction just as fast when you manage it with intention.

Section 8: Scoring Models: FICO vs. VantageScore

Not every score you see is the score a lender uses. That is one of the most frustrating realities for consumers. FICO and VantageScore are both legitimate scoring models, but lenders often prioritize FICO in mortgage decisions, while many consumer-facing tools show VantageScore. This creates confusion when a borrower monitors one score and gets priced off another.

The right way to think about scoring models is not "which one is real," but "which one is being used in the decision I am making." If you are preparing for a mortgage, you want to understand mortgage-focused scoring and the Middle Credit Score method. If you are working on general credit health, monitoring trends across models still helps because strong habits improve both over time.

From My Client Files - Example 8 (Chapter 1): Navigating Scoring Models

---

Melissa was frustrated because her credit scores did not line up across different lenders. One lender showed her qualifying comfortably, while another treated her profile as higher risk. It felt inconsistent and unfair until we stepped back and looked at what was happening behind the scenes. Different lenders were using different scoring models, each interpreting her utilization and recent activity through a slightly different lens and time frame.

Once Melissa understood that scoring models do not just measure behavior, but patterns over time, her approach changed. She stopped reacting to individual score swings and focused instead on creating steady, predictable habits like keeping utilization low consistently and avoiding short-term spikes. What initially felt like confusion became clarity. And that clarity turned into strategy, a strategy that produced stable scores, better terms, and confidence moving forward.

Section 9: The Role of the Middle Credit Score

The Middle Credit Score is a gamechanger because it becomes the anchor point for major lending decisions. It is the score that often determines whether you're offered top-tier terms or placed in a more expensive bucket. It is also the score most likely to surprise borrowers who monitor only one bureau or assume the highest score will carry the day.

If your scores are 680, 710, and 750, the lender is not pricing you off 750. They are pricing you off 710. That reality is what makes the Middle Credit Score worth mastering. Once you understand it, you stop wasting energy on wishful thinking and start focusing on the moves that reliably improve the score that matters.

From My Client Files - Example 9 (Chapter 1): Balanced Credit Success

Sandra assumed her highest credit score would carry the most weight in lending decisions. Like many consumers, she focused on the number that looked best and didn't realize that lenders often rely on the middle score when evaluating risk and pricing. When her application did not produce the terms she expected, she felt blindsided until we reviewed her reports together and identified that one bureau was quietly dragging her profile down.

Once Sandra understood what mattered, her strategy became focused and effective. She disputed outdated information that no longer belonged on her report and addressed utilization in a way that created balance across all three bureaus. The result was not just a higher score; it was a shift into a better pricing tier. That shift is where the real savings live - lower interest, better terms, and long-term financial leverage.

Section 10: Deep Understanding

- Mortgage underwriting relies on the median, not the best-case score
- The middle score often determines pricing tiers and loan approval strength
- Monitoring one bureau can create false confidence or unnecessary fear
- Optimizing the middle score requires accuracy, balance, and timing

Section 11: Why the Middle Credit Score Matters

The Middle Credit Score matters because it is where fairness and consequence collide. It is fair because it reduces the influence of an outlier score. It is consequential because the difference between tiers is expensive. People do not lose money because they "did not qualify." They lose money because they qualified at the wrong price.

This is why the Middle Credit Score is empowering. Once you understand that the system is seeking stability and consistency across all three bureaus, you stop treating credit as a mystery and start treating it as a measurable project. And that project pays you back, month after month, through better terms.

5 Actionable Steps to Avoid

1. Assuming your highest score will be used
2. Monitoring only one bureau and missing a significant discrepancy
3. Letting utilization rise before applying "just for a month" (reduce spending)
4. Closing old accounts without understanding the impact on history and utilization
5. Applying for new credit right before a major loan decision

Chapter 1 Closing: What Credit Really Decides

If there is one mistake, I have watched people make repeatedly, it is assuming credit is something you deal with later. Later, when income is higher. Later, when life is more stable. Later, when you are "ready." The truth is, credit is already working quietly setting prices, limiting options, and deciding outcomes long before you sit across from a lender or landlord.

The Middle Credit Score exists because the system values consistency over perfection. It doesn't reward extremes. It rewards patterns. That is good news for anyone willing to learn how the system works. When you understand what the score measures and why the middle number matters most, you stop reacting and start planning. You stop hoping and start positioning.

This chapter was not meant to overwhelm you. It was meant to give you clarity. Credit is not a judgment of who you are, it reflects what you have done and how recently you have done it. Once you understand that, credit becomes manageable, predictable, and ultimately helpful. The rest of this book builds on that foundation.

The One Action Framework

The "Middle Credit Score Foundation" Plan (30 / 60 / 90 Days)

Days 1–30: Stabilize and Verify
Pull all three credit reports and compare them line by line. Identify inconsistencies, outdated items, duplicate accounts, and unfamiliar activity. Bring awareness to utilization not by guessing, but by seeing exactly where balances sit across accounts.

Days 31–60: Optimize the Levers That Move the Score
Strategically reduce revolving balances to improve utilization across bureaus. Protect payment history with a zero-tolerance policy for late payments. Avoid new inquiries unless necessary. Continue dispute follow-ups until corrections are confirmed and posted.

Days 61–90: Prepare Like an Underwriter Will Review You
Make your profile boring in the best way possible: stable balances, clean payments, no new credit activity, accurate reporting, and

consistency across bureaus. This is where many borrowers lose momentum and become impatient. Discipline here is what separates average outcomes from optimal ones.

Chapter 1 Final Takeaways

- Credit scores are pricing tools, not identity labels
- The Middle Credit Score often determines mortgage approval strength and cost
- Consistency matters more than intensity because small habits compound
- Monitoring and correcting reports prevents expensive surprises
- Utilization and timing can change outcomes even when income stays the same

The Middle Credit Score®

The Gold Standard for Financial Decisions

When I first started originating loans, I quickly realized that most
borrowers viewed credit the way people look at school grades:
they wanted to talk about their best score. If they saw a 740
anywhere, they assumed that was the number that mattered. And
if they saw a 640 anywhere, they assumed the game was over.
They were not wrong to care because the reality is that credit
scores absolutely shape your financial life, but they were focused
on the bad part of the picture. In the lending world, we do not
underwrite the extremes. We underwrite the middle credit score.

That number is your **Middle Credit Score®**, and it is the quiet authority behind most major lending decisions. It is called "middle" because it is the median score pulled from the three major bureaus: Experian, Equifax, and TransUnion. Not the highest. Not the lowest. The middle. That one score becomes the standard lenders lean on because it is the most consistent and least susceptible to distortion. It filters out the oddball swings that occur when one bureau updates late, reports an account differently, or contains an error that doesn't exist elsewhere.

Over the years, I have watched the Middle Credit Score® determine who gets approved, who gets denied, and just as important, who gets the expensive loan version versus the affordable one. A borrower can technically qualify with a lower score, but the cost of that loan can change the entire homeownership experience. If you have ever wondered why one person pays hundreds less per month for what looks like the same home, the exact purchase price, and the same loan term, a big part of the answer often lives in this single metric.

This chapter is about more than explaining what the Middle Credit Score is. It's about showing you why it matters, how lenders use it, and how you can use it to protect your future. Because once you understand the middle score, you stop playing guessing games. You stop chasing the wrong number. And you start building the kind of credit profile that gives you options that save you money and provide you with leverage.

Section 1: The Mechanics of the Middle Credit Score®

The Middle Credit Score is the most straightforward concept in lending that most consumers never hear explained clearly. When a lender pulls credit, they do not see a single score, they see three. The reality is that those three scores rarely match perfectly. Each bureau may be working with slightly different data. Some creditors report to all three; some report to only one or two. Balances update at various times. Disputes can temporarily alter a file. A collection might show on one bureau but not another. It is messy, and that is precisely why lenders use a method designed to create stability.

To calculate the Middle Credit Score, you line up the three bureau scores from lowest to highest and choose the one in the middle. If your scores are 680, 700, and 720, the middle score is 700. That is it. It is not an average. It is not a weighted formula. It is simply the median, and in lending, that median becomes a decision-making anchor.

Now here is the part most people do not understand until they are sitting in front of an estimate they did not expect: the Middle Credit Score is not just used to decide *if* you qualify. It is often used to determine *how much you will pay*. That means it influences interest rates, lender pricing adjustments, and, in many cases, the total fees required to close. The difference between a "good enough" score and a "strong" score can manifest as higher monthly payments, higher lifetime interest costs, and fewer program options.

What makes the middle score so powerful is that it prevents one bureau from unfairly controlling the outcome, but it also means you cannot hide behind your best score. You cannot point to the highest number and say, "Use that one." The system is designed to be consistent, and that consistency is what lenders trust. If you want better terms, you must strengthen the Middle Credit Score®, because that is what underwriting will lean on when it is time to price your loan.

From My Client Files - Example 10 (Chapter 2): Difference Between "Best Score" and "Lender Score"

Mary was a nurse who did everything right in life such as having steady work, steady income, responsible habits. When she came to me, she was ready to buy her first home and proud of her credit. She told me her score was over 700, and she was not lying. One of her bureau scores was a 720. But when the lender priced her loan, the terms reflected something slightly lower than she expected.

When we reviewed her file, her scores were 680, 700, and 720. Her focus was on the 720. Underwriting focused on the 700. That's the Middle Credit Score. Once she understood that, we stopped guessing and started working strategically. We looked for the difference-maker and found it: an incorrectly reported late payment dragging down one bureau. She had documentation showing the account was paid as agreed. She filed a dispute with supporting proof. Within weeks, the bureau corrected the entry, her lower score moved upward, and her Middle Credit Score climbed high enough to shift her into a better pricing range.

*Mary did not just "feel better" after that correction, she **saved real money**. Over the life of her mortgage, that adjustment translated into savings that would have otherwise gone straight to interest. That is the moment many borrowers have: when they realize credit is not just about identity or pride, it is about cost.*

Actionable Steps: How to Identify and Optimize the Score Lenders Actually Use:

1. **Pull All Three Bureau Scores, Not Just One**
   Do not rely on a single score from a monitoring app. Request or review your Experian, Equifax, and TransUnion scores side by side so you can see the full range lenders will evaluate.

2. **Identify the Middle Credit Score®**
   Line the three scores up from lowest to highest and focus on the middle number. This is the score many mortgage lenders use to price loans and determine eligibility tiers.

3. **Compare What's Dragging One Bureau Down**
   Look for discrepancies: a late payment showing on one bureau but not the others, outdated balances, incorrect account statuses, or reporting delays.

4. **Verify Before You Dispute**
   If you believe an item is inaccurate, gather documentation first that include payment confirmations, statements, or correspondence. Accuracy wins disputes faster than emotion.

5. **Dispute Strategically, Not Broadly**
   File a targeted dispute only for verified errors. Avoid disputing accurate items or flooding bureaus with unnecessary claims, which can delay resolution.

6. **Monitor the Correction Across Bureaus**
   Once corrected, confirm that the update posts properly and that your Middle Credit Score® reflects the change. Do not assume one bureau update automatically fixes the others.

7. **Translate Score Improvement Into Cost Awareness**
   Re-run loan pricing once the Middle Credit Score® improves. Understand how even a small tier shift can reduce interest rates, monthly payments, and long-term cost.

Section 2: Why Lenders Prioritize the Middle Credit Score

Lenders do not use the Middle Credit Score to be complicated. They use it because they are managing risk at scale. A mortgage is a long-term bet. An auto loan is still a multi-year commitment. Lending decisions are made with the understanding that the borrower's behavior today must predict their behavior for years to come. That's why lenders value consistency and reliability over extremes.

The highest score can be misleading, as it may reflect missing data or limited reporting. The lowest score can be misleading, as it may reflect a one-time error, a late update, or a bureau-specific dispute. The middle score reduces the likelihood that a single glitch or timing issue will distort the lender's view. In other words, lenders trust the middle score because it is the most stable compromise between three different reporting systems.

That stability becomes especially important when underwriting is automated, where score thresholds can instantly change pricing. The system does not care that your highest score is strong if your middle score is below a key tier. The algorithm will price the loan based on what it is designed to trust, and that is most often the median.

For you, the borrower, this is both good news and bad news. The good news is that the middle score protects you from being judged solely by a single bureau's error. The bad news is you cannot pretend the low bureau does not exist. The middle score forces you to keep your credit healthy across the board. That is why monitoring all three bureaus matters, and that is why strategic credit improvement focuses on the median, not the vanity score you like best.

Borrower Blind Spot: Why So Many People Miss the Middle

One of the most common patterns I have seen over the years is not that borrowers have bad credit, it's that they misunderstand how their credit is being evaluated. Most consumers are never taught how lenders read a credit file. They are shown scores, alerts, colors, and charts, but not context. As a result, they focus on the loudest number instead of the most important one.

Consumer-facing credit tools reinforce this confusion. They highlight a single score, often updated frequently, and frame movement as progress or failure. What they do not explain is that lenders are not reacting to daily score fluctuations. They are evaluating patterns, and more importantly, they are anchoring decisions to the Middle Credit Score®, not the number that happens to look best that week.

I have sat across from borrowers who were genuinely shocked when their loan pricing did not match what they expected. Not angry, simply confused. They had been "doing the right things" according to what they were shown. They paid on time. They watched their app. They avoided obvious mistakes. What they did not realize was that a small imbalance such as a higher balance reported on one bureau, and an old account misreported on another, was quietly pulling their middle credit score into a lower tier.

This blind spot is dangerous because it creates false confidence. Borrowers assume they are prepared because one score looks strong, when in reality the median is fragile, and fragility is what lenders price for. A Middle Credit Score that sits just below a key threshold can cost more than most people expect, even when everything else about the loan looks solid.

The most empowering shift I see in clients happens when they stop asking, "What's my score today?" and start asking, "What does my full profile look like across all three bureaus?" That question changes behavior. It leads to better timing, smarter balance management, and fewer surprises. It replaces anxiety with strategy.

Once borrowers understand this, their relationship with credit changes. They stop reacting emotionally to score movement and start managing credit like an asset. That mindset, not perfection, is what consistently leads to better outcomes.

Section 3: The Real-Life Cost of the Middle Credit Score

Credit scores are often discussed like they are abstract, like they are just a number. But in lending, your credit score behaves more like a price tag. The cost difference between the two middle scores is not theoretical. It can appear on your payment every single month. It can seem like Private Mortgage Insurance (PMI). It can show up as points at closing, which can make a lifetime difference, adding up to tens of thousands of dollars.

I have seen borrowers qualify for the same loan amount, with the same down payment, buying similar homes, and walk away with entirely different loan costs simply because their Middle Credit Score placed them in a different tier. One borrower thinks, "I got approved, so I'm good." But the stronger borrower thinks, "I got approved, *and* I got the affordable version of the loan." That difference is the gap between surviving a mortgage and building wealth through it.

This is not just for mortgages because lenders that provide auto loans price borrowers the same way. A Middle Credit Score can push you into a higher interest range, turning a reasonable purchase into an unnecessarily expensive one. Personal loans, credit cards, and consolidation products are priced the same way, and your costs are often anchored to the median score that reduces bureau-specific distortions.

Here is what you should walk away with: the Middle Credit Score is not just a lender's preference. It is a financial lever, and when you improve it, you are not just improving a number, you are improving your cost of money.

Section 4: What the Middle Credit Score Says About Your Financial Health

Your Middle Credit Score is a summary of your financial habits. It is not judging your character; it is measuring patterns. It reflects how often you pay on time, how heavily you rely on revolving credit, how stable your accounts are over time, and how frequently you apply for new credit. It is a snapshot of your financial behavior under pressure.

One of the fastest ways to influence that snapshot is credit utilization. Utilization is the percentage of your available revolving credit that you are using. High utilization signals risk because it suggests dependence on credit and limited financial flexibility. Even if you pay on time, high utilization can suppress your scores. On the other hand, low utilization signals control. That is why borrowers preparing for a mortgage often see score gains by paying down balances, not because they became different people, but because their profile became less risky.

What lenders want is predictability. A clean payment history, low utilization, stable accounts, and limited new inquiries suggest you will continue paying as agreed. That is what a strong middle score represents, stability.

Section 5: Middle Credit Score vs. Other Scores Consumers See

Most consumers do not realize they are viewing credit through a different lens than lenders do. Consumer apps often show a single score, sometimes from a single bureau, and frequently use a model that differs from the one mortgage lenders use. That can create false confidence or unnecessary panic.

The Middle Credit Score is different because it is not about convenience, it is about underwriting accuracy. It is a standard created for lenders to make long-term decisions responsibly, and because it is the median, it reduces the distortion caused by one unusually high or low bureau score. If you only monitor one score, you can be blindsided. If you monitor all three, you can proactively manage your profile and avoid surprises.

This is one of the biggest mindset shifts borrowers need: do not ask, "What is my credit score?" Ask, "What are my three bureau scores, and what is my Middle Credit Score®?"

Section 6: Why Monitoring All Three Bureaus Matters

Monitoring all three bureaus is not about obsession, it is about protection. Credit reporting errors happen more often than people think, such as duplicate accounts, incorrect balances, outdated statuses, mixed files, identity issues, or a creditor reporting late when you paid on time. When you monitor only one bureau, you can miss the error that controls your middle score.

If you are months away from buying a home, you do not want to discover a problem the week your lender pulls credit. You want to learn it early enough to dispute it, correct it, and allow the bureaus to update their records. Credit repair, or real credit correction, is often a game of timing. The earlier you see the issue, the more power you have to fix it.

Section 7: Practical Steps to Strengthen Your Middle Credit Score

Improving your Middle Credit Score does not require perfection, it requires focus. In most cases, the fastest improvements come from three areas: lowering utilization, cleaning up reporting errors, and building an uninterrupted streak of on-time payments.

The process is not glamorous. It is consistent. You reduce balances and keep them low. You stop triggering hard inquiries. You correct inaccuracies with documentation. You automate payments, so life does not create a late mark. You let time do its work while you maintain stable behavior.

Here is something I have learned: borrowers often underestimate how robust stability is. When you stop causing fluctuations and start managing your profile like a long-term asset, your Middle Credit Score becomes less fragile. That is when you gain leverage.

Section 8: Leveraging Your Middle Credit Score

A strong Middle Credit Score gives you power in the lending conversation. It changes how lenders view you. It changes what products open-up. It can reduce fees. It can reduce PMI costs. It can improve refinancing options. It can enhance debt consolidation terms. It can influence your ability to purchase investment property. It can shape the speed and smoothness of underwriting.

When your score is strong, you negotiate from a position of strength. When your score is borderline, you negotiate from defense. The goal is not just to be approved. The goal is to secure terms that help you build wealth rather than drain it.

10 High-Impact Actions That Move the Middle Score

1. Pull all three bureau reports and identify your median score.

2. Dispute errors with documentation immediately.
3. Bring utilization under 30% (under 10% if prepping for a mortgage).
4. Avoid new credit applications for 90 days before underwriting.
5. Keep old accounts open when possible.
6. Set autopay for minimums and manual-pay for strategy.
7. Pay revolving balances before statement cut dates.
8. Consolidate rate-shopping into a short window.
9. Track score changes monthly as you approach a significant loan.
10. Focus on improving the score that controls the median, not the score that makes you feel best.

Section 9: The Transformative Power of a Strong Middle Credit Score® - Real Life Examples

Over the years, I have seen one truth repeat itself again and again: the Middle Credit Score quietly determines who builds wealth faster and who unknowingly pays a premium just to borrow money. The difference is rarely dramatic on paper at first glance. It often shows up as a fraction of a percentage point on an interest rate or a slightly higher monthly payment. But when those minor differences are stretched over years or decades, they can add up to tens, sometimes hundreds, of thousands of dollars.

I often explain it to clients this way: two borrowers can walk into a lender's office with similar incomes, similar savings, and similar goals, yet leave with vastly different financial outcomes. The dividing line is usually not income or ambition. It is the Middle Credit Score®.

Consider two borrowers purchasing the same $300,000 home. One has a Middle Credit Score of 740 and qualifies for a lower interest rate. The other, with a score of 670, is offered a higher rate. On the surface, that difference may not feel life changing. But over the life of the loan, it becomes exactly that. One borrower builds equity faster, keeps monthly payments manageable, and retains flexibility. The other commits to nearly $105,000 more in interest which is money that never builds wealth, compounds, or comes back.

This pattern does not only show up in mortgages. I have worked with first-time buyers who assumed homeownership was out of reach simply because their initial rate quote felt overwhelming. In one case, a buyer with a Middle Credit Score just under 700 accepted a higher rate because they did not understand how close they were to a better tier. With targeted adjustments like paying down revolving balances, and avoiding new inquiries, that same buyer crossed the next threshold within months. The result was not just a lower rate, but a shift in confidence. The numbers finally worked, and the dream became achievable.

Auto loans tell the same story in a shorter time frame. I have seen borrowers finance identical vehicles at dramatically different costs, purely because one Middle Credit Score crossed a key boundary, and the other did not. A stronger score turns a routine purchase into a manageable expense. A weaker one quietly inflates transportation costs for years.

Business owners often feel this impact even more acutely. Expansion capital is expensive when creditworthiness lags ambition. I have watched entrepreneurs pour profits into interest payments instead of equipment, staff, or marketing, all because their Middle Credit Score put them in a higher-risk category. When those same owners took the time to correct reporting errors and rebalance utilization, the shift was immediate. Capital became a tool instead of a burden.

Even costs that do not feel like "loans," such as private mortgage insurance, are heavily influenced by this one metric. I have advised clients to pause major decisions, not because they were not ready, but because a short delay allowed them to eliminate PMI. The savings were not theoretical. They were real, monthly, and permanent.

What all these examples have in common is not perfection. None of these borrowers started with flawless credit. They started with awareness. Once they understood how the Middle Credit Score worked and how lenders used it, their decisions became strategic rather than reactive. That shift alone often made the difference.

Section 9 Recap: What These Stories Reveal

- The Middle Credit Score quietly controls how expensive borrowing becomes over time
- Minor score differences compound into massive long-term costs or savings
- Timing matters because modest improvements before applying can permanently change outcomes
- Credit strength creates flexibility, not just approval
- Awareness turns credit from an obstacle into a financial tool

Section 10: Avoiding Common Mistakes That Hurt Your Middle Credit Score

Most damage to a Middle Credit Score does not come from reckless behavior. It comes from well-intentioned decisions made without understanding how credit scoring works. I have seen borrowers do everything "right" in their minds, only to be blindsided when their score drops at the worst possible moment.

One of the most common mistakes is treating credit card utilization as a temporary issue. Borrowers often assume that carrying a high balance for a short period won't matter if it is paid off quickly. Utilization snapshots are taken monthly. Even brief spikes can lower a score enough to affect loan terms, especially if an application follows shortly afterward.

Another frequent misstep is closing older accounts in the name of simplicity. From a consumer perspective, this feels responsible for fewer cards, fewer worries. From a scoring perspective, it often shortens credit history while raising utilization. I have seen scores drop not because of debt, but because history disappeared.

Then there is the quiet damage caused by neglect. Credit reports are not self-correcting documents. Errors linger. Duplicate accounts, outdated balances, and incorrect payment statuses do not resolve themselves. When borrowers do not monitor all three bureaus, these mistakes compound invisibly until a lender pulls the report, and the consequences become unavoidable.

Application timing is another area where good intentions backfire. Applying for multiple forms of credit close together, outside of a protected rate-shopping window, can create a perception of financial stress. Even borrowers with strong histories can temporarily weaken their Middle Credit Score by applying impulsively rather than strategically.

I have worked with clients who could have avoided higher rates, denials, or delays simply by understanding these patterns in advance. Credit damage is rarely sudden. It accumulates quietly, and often unnecessarily.

5 Actionable Steps to Avoid: The Most Common Middle Credit Score Pitfalls

1. Letting credit utilization spike, even temporarily, before applying
2. Closing long-standing accounts without understanding the impact on history
3. Ignoring credit reports until a lender reviews them
4. Applying for multiple credit products outside of strategic windows
5. Assuming paid-off debts automatically update across all bureaus

Chapter 2 Closing: The Score That Actually Sets the Price

Most consumers spend years chasing the highest number they can find on a screen, without ever being told which number matters when real financial decisions are made. That confusion is not accidental; it is the result of a system that was never designed to educate the consumer, only to score them. The Middle Credit Score cuts through that confusion. It is not about perfection, and it is not about bragging rights. It's about consistency, reliability, and how lenders measure risk when real money is on the line.

What I have seen over decades in lending and real estate is simple: borrowers do not lose opportunities because they lack effort; they lose them because they were aiming at the wrong target. Understanding the Middle Credit Score shifts your focus from obsession to control. Instead of reacting to every score fluctuation, you begin to focus on what moves outcomes: clean reporting across all three bureaus, controlled utilization, stable behavior, and predictable trends. That shift alone can change how you experience credit entirely.

This chapter was not written to make you monitor your credit more often; it was written to help you monitor it more intelligently. Once you understand why the Middle Credit Score exists and how it is used, you stop guessing. You stop being surprised, and you stop letting a system you do not understand dictate your financial confidence. From here forward, credit becomes something you manage with clarity instead of something you fear, chase, or misunderstand.

The One Action Framework

The "Middle Credit Score Awareness" Plan (30 / 60 / 90 Days)

Days 1–30: Observe & Compare
Pull all three bureau reports and determine your accurate Middle Credit Score. Review each bureau line by line to identify discrepancies, outdated information, or utilization imbalances that may be suppressing the median.

Days 31–60: Identify Inconsistencies

Reduce revolving balances strategically, focusing on accounts reported across multiple bureaus. Dispute documented errors that affect the lowest score. Avoid new inquiries and stabilize account behavior so the median score has room to rise.

Days 61–90: Stop relying on single-score apps

Maintain low utilization, flawless payment history, and zero unnecessary credit activity. Allow time for updates to post across bureaus. This is the phase when patience protects pricing and when most borrowers make mistakes by moving too soon.

Chapter 2 Final Takeaways

- Lenders price loans using the median, not the highest score
- Slight differences in the Middle Credit Score compound into high long-term costs
- Monitoring all three bureaus prevents pricing surprises
- Utilization and timing matter more than people realize
- Improving the middle score is the fastest way to reduce the cost of money

3

Building and Maintaining a Strong Credit Profile

Credit Strength Is Built, Not Given

When I started as a lender, one thing became clear very quickly: most people had no idea how fragile or powerful their credit profile really was. I watched borrowers with solid incomes and good intentions lose opportunities simply because they did not understand how credit worked behind the scenes. I also saw the opposite: people with average incomes and modest resources build extraordinary financial leverage by learning to manage credit with intention.

Your credit profile is not just a reflection of what you have done. It is a signal of how you handle responsibility over time. It tells lenders, landlords, insurers, and financial institutions how predictable you are, and predictability is what earns you better terms. A strong credit profile lowers friction in your life. It gives you options. It saves you money quietly, month after month, often without you even realizing it.

Over the last three decades, I have worked with thousands of consumers at every stage of the credit spectrum, from those starting with no history at all, to those rebuilding after serious setbacks. What I have learned is this: building and maintaining strong credit is not about perfection. It is about understanding the rules and playing the long game with discipline. In this chapter, I will walk you through what matters, what does not, and how to build a credit profile that supports your goals instead of standing in your way.

Section 1: The Foundation of a Strong Credit Profile

A strong credit profile is built the same way trust is built slowly, consistently, and through repeated behavior. Lenders don't expect perfection, but they do expect predictability. When they look at your credit profile, they're trying to answer a straightforward question: Can this person be relied upon to manage borrowed money responsibly over time?

Payment history sits at the center of that evaluation. It is the clearest indicator of reliability. When payments are made on time, month after month, it sends a powerful message that you honor your obligations. One missed payment, especially if it is recent, can undo months of progress because it introduces uncertainty into your profile. That is why consistency matters more than speed when it comes to improving credit.

Credit utilization tells another part of the story. Even when payments are on time, high balances relative to limits can signal financial strain. I've seen many borrowers shocked to learn that paying the minimum isn't enough to protect their profile. Utilization is not about whether you can make payments; it is about how close you are to your limits. Lower balances communicate control. Higher balances suggest risk, even if income is high.

The final piece of the foundation is the credit mix. This does not mean opening accounts just to check boxes. It means demonstrating that you can responsibly manage different forms of credit over time. Revolving accounts show restraint. Installment loans show commitment. Together, they add depth and credibility to your profile. When these elements work together, they create a foundation that supports long-term financial flexibility.

Section 2: Building the Foundation the Right Way

From My Client Files - Example 11 (Chapter 3): High Credit Utilization

---

Mina came to me determined to buy her first home but frustrated by the terms she was being offered. On paper, she looked fine. She had a stable income, savings, and no major red flags. But when we reviewed her credit profile closely, the weaknesses were apparent. A missed payment from months earlier still lingered. Her credit cards carried balances that pushed her utilization higher than she realized, and her profile relied almost entirely on revolving credit.

What Mina needed wasn't a miracle; she required structure. We started with payment consistency, locking in automatic payments so nothing slipped through again. From there, we focused on utilization, creating a targeted plan to bring balances down, rather than spreading payments thin. Finally, we added a small installment account to round out her profile, which she managed carefully and paid exactly as agreed.

The change didn't happen overnight, but it didn't take years either. Within a few months, Mina's Middle Credit Score® moved into a stronger tier. More importantly, her profile now told a different story, one of control, reliability, and intention. When she reapplied for her mortgage, the terms finally matched the borrower she was. That's the power of building credit deliberately instead of passively.

Section 3: Recovering From Financial Setbacks Sets the Stage for Rebuilding with Resilience

Financial setbacks are part of life. Job losses, medical emergencies, and unexpected expenses can hit even the most responsible people. What separates those who recover from those who stay stuck is not the setback itself; it's how quickly and deliberately they respond.

When someone is rebuilding credit, the priority is containment. That means stopping further damage by addressing delinquent accounts and re-establishing on-time payments wherever possible. Bringing accounts current, negotiating payment arrangements, or resolving collections does not erase the past, but it prevents the future from getting worse. From there, consistency becomes the most powerful tool available.

I have seen rebuilding work best when people focus on small, controllable actions. A secured credit card used sparingly and paid in full can rebuild trust surprisingly fast. When managed correctly, credit-builder loans reinforce positive behavior. Disputing legitimate errors can immediately reduce a profile's weight. None of these steps is dramatic on its own, but together they signal recovery and stability.

From My Client Files - Example 12 (Chapter 3): Rebuilding After a Breakdown

---

Debbie's situation changed overnight when medical bills disrupted her finances. Missed payments followed, then collections, and soon her credit profile no longer reflected who she was trying to become. When we met, she was overwhelmed and embarrassed, emotions I see far too often in people who simply fell into challenging circumstances.

We approached her recovery methodically. First, we contacted creditors and stabilized outstanding accounts. Then we rebuilt her payment history using a secured card she treated like cash. She became disciplined about monitoring her reports and disputing inaccuracies, including a duplicate collection that never should have been there. Month by month, her profile began to heal.

Within six months, her Middle Credit Score® had climbed meaningfully. Within a year, she was preparing to become a homeowner again. What changed wasn't just her credit; it was her confidence. She stopped seeing credit as punishment and began to see it as a system she could navigate.

Section 4: The Role of Credit Monitoring

Credit monitoring is one of those habits people don't respect until something goes wrong. I've had clients tell me, "Glenn, I did not think I needed to check my credit because I pay my bills." And I get it, that sounds logical, but credit is not just about what you *do* with your money. It is also about what gets *reported* about your money, and those two things do not always match.

Your credit reports are living documents. Accounts update. Balances change. Remarks get added. Sometimes errors appear and sit there for months, quietly lowering your score until the day you apply for something important, and you find out the hard way. Monitoring protects you from that moment. It keeps you aware, not anxious. In my world, it's the difference between being prepared and being surprised.

Monitoring also gives you feedback. When you pay down a balance, you should be able to see how it impacts your utilization. When you dispute an error, you should know whether it was corrected and whether the bureau updated it across the right fields. When you're building momentum, monitoring becomes motivation because progress becomes visible. You cannot stay committed to what you cannot track.

Now we will address fraud. We live in a world where your identity can be used without your permission faster than you can imagine. I have seen consumers lose months, even years, trying to unwind accounts they never opened. That is why I look at monitoring as a security system. Not because you're paranoid. Because you're responsible.

The goal is not to obsess. The goal is to **own your file**. When your credit file is clean, accurate, and up to date, your Middle Credit Score becomes a reliable reflection of who you really are financially, and that puts the power back where it belongs: in your hands.

Section 5: Balancing Short-Term Wins and Long-Term Credit Power

One of the biggest mistakes I see is people chasing quick fixes without a long-term strategy or committing to the long term without cleaning up the short-term mess. Credit doesn't reward extremes. It rewards balance. If you treat credit like a sprint, you will burn out. If you treat it like something you will "get to one day," you will miss opportunities. The real game is learning how to do both at the same time.

Short-term wins matter because they create breathing room. Paying down a maxed-out card can quickly improve your utilization. Catching up on a past-due account stops the bleeding. Correcting a reporting error can give you an immediate lift. These are the moves that get your profile back into a healthier lane, and when you need credit soon, they can be the difference between "approved" and "not approved," or between an interest rate tier that helps you and one that punishes you.

However, long-term credit power is what changes your life. That is where people either build wealth with leverage or keep paying the "high-cost tax" for years. Long-term credit power comes from consistency, account age, stability, and restraint; the kind of behaviors that tell lenders you're not a risk today *and you won't be a risk tomorrow.* That is why the long game includes keeping older accounts open, spacing out applications, and thinking ahead before major purchases.

If you want my truth on this: credit is less about what you know and more about what you repeat. The system rewards patterns. It punishes chaos. When you balance short-term cleanup with long-term discipline, your Middle Credit Score does not just improve, it stabilizes. And stability is what gets rewarded.

From My Client Files - Example 13 (Chapter 3): When Short-Term Fixes Aren't Enough

---

Danielle came to me feeling proud, and she should have been. She had recently paid off a medical collection that was weighing down her profile. That's not easy. It takes sacrifice and courage. But after all that effort, her score still wasn't moving the way she expected. She told me, "I thought once that collection was gone, everything would bounce back."

When we looked deeper, the issue was not a single old problem; it was a daily pattern. Her credit cards were still running high, and her utilization stayed elevated month after month. On top of that, she was considering closing her oldest account because she no longer used it. That would have made her credit history shorter and her utilization worse at the same time, the exact opposite of what she needed.

We rebuilt her strategy with balance. The short-term plan focused on utilization: targeted payments, a structured payoff schedule, and no new charges while she was reducing balances. The long-term plan protected her history: we kept the old account open and active with a small monthly recurring payment. We also added one carefully selected installment account to strengthen her mix, not because she needed debt, but because she needed a stronger profile.

*Within a year, her Middle Credit Score was not only higher but also healthier. Danielle stopped "fixing credit" and started **building credit**. That mindset shift is what changed everything.*

Section 6: Maintaining Momentum for Credit Success

I tell people this all the time: getting your credit up is one thing. Keeping it strong is the real flex. Because life doesn't pause just because your score improved. Expenses come. Temptations come. Emergencies happen. And credit has a way of slipping when you stop paying attention.

Maintaining momentum means treating your credit as something you manage, not as something you hope stays good. It's like physical health. You don't work out for three months, hit your goal, and then decide fitness is over. Credit works the same way. It's maintained through routine: consistent payments, low utilization, careful borrowing decisions, and periodic check-ins.

This is also where people start making dangerous assumptions. They will say, "My score is great, so I can do whatever." That's when they finance furniture, open multiple cards for points, let balances creep, and take hard inquiries they didn't need. Most of the time, nothing happens right away, which makes them believe it's fine. Until the day they need a mortgage, a refinance, a business loan, or rental approval, those "small" decisions suddenly show up like a bill.

Momentum is built by alignment. Your credit habits should match your goals. If your goal is homeownership, your profile should be stable, clean, and boring. If your goal is debt freedom, your utilization should be dropping, and your payment history should be flawless. If your goal is wealth building, your credit should be positioned to give you leverage at the right time, not pressure at the wrong time.

Credit success doesn't come from being perfect. It comes from being consistent enough, long enough that lenders see you as safe, and safety is what earns lower rates, better approvals, and better outcomes.

From My Client Files - Example 14 (Chapter 3): Establishing Credit When You Have No History

---

Alex came out of college with ambition, discipline, and steady income, but no credit history. And that's the part most people don't understand. You can be responsible, organized, and financially cautious and still be invisible to the credit system. The system doesn't reward intent. It rewards evidence. And without reported behavior, lenders don't see potential, they see uncertainty. That invisibility doesn't just delay opportunities; it quietly limits them.

Instead of rushing into multiple accounts or chasing shortcuts, Alex took a deliberate approach. He started with a secured credit card, not as a "beginner step," but as a controlled strategy. He treated the card like a reporting tool, not a spending license. He used it for small, predictable expenses, kept utilization low, and paid the balance in full every cycle. Month after month, he repeated the same disciplined pattern. No spikes. No missed payments. No noise. Just consistency.

Over time, that consistency created what the credit system requires most: a track record. As positive behavior reported across the bureaus, Alex's Middle Credit

Score climbed into a range where lenders could evaluate him. The real win wasn't the number, it was visibility. He moved from being ignored to being assessed, and once you're assessable, options appear. That's the lesson: credit doesn't measure who you are, it measures what you've proven.

From My Client Files - Example 15 (Chapter 3): Strengthening a Profile by Fixing Utilization

---

Emily had credit, but her utilization was choking her progress. She wasn't reckless; she was simply carrying balances that made her look stressed on paper. And credit does not ask why; it reports on the behavior and scores it.

She did two things that changed her situation: she attacked the balances with intention, and she improved her ratio. That meant focusing on the cards with the highest utilization first, not just the ones with the highest interest rates. It also meant making changes that would shift the math in her favor, like requesting a credit limit increase only when it made sense and only when she knew she could keep her behavior stable.

Within months, her Middle Credit Score improved not because she became a different person, but because her profile finally reflected the discipline she already had. That's what utilization does. It can hide your strength or highlight it, depending on how you manage it.

From My Client Files - Example 16 (Chapter 3): Recovering from One Missed Payment

---

Jordan missed a payment while traveling, one mistake. No pattern. No chronic issue. But credit scoring does not care that you were on vacation. It cares that the payment was late.

Here is what mattered: Jordan acted immediately. He called the issuer, explained the situation honestly, and requested a goodwill adjustment based on his history. Sometimes that works, sometimes it does not, but you do not know until you ask. Then he protected the future by automating payments so the mistake could not repeat itself.

Over the next several months, his score recovered. The lesson here is not "never make mistakes." The lesson is: when mistakes happen, respond like a professional. Credit recovery is often about speed and consistency after the incident.

From My Client Files - Example 17 (Chapter 3): Rebuilding After Financial Collapse

Marie's story is the one I've seen too many times. She lost her job, then the bills stacked up, then credit cards went past due, and then collections followed. People judge that chain of events like it is a character flaw, but it is often a circumstance problem that becomes a credit problem.

Her rebuild started with honesty and structure. She negotiated what could be negotiated, resolved what could be resolved, and stopped trying to fix everything at once. Then she rebuilt the foundation with a secured card, on-time payments, and low balances. Over time, the system responded. It always does. Not overnight, but reliably.

Marie's score improved because her behavior improved, and her behavior improved because she had a plan. That is the formula I want readers to understand; credit restoration is not magic. It is organized consistency.

From My Client Files - Example 18 (Chapter 3):
Maintaining Excellent Credit Before a Major Move

David did not wait for a mortgage application to start caring about his credit, he treated preparation as part of the process. His profile was already solid, but he understood that major financial moves demand stability, not activity. As he prepared for homeownership, he avoided unnecessary credit inquiries, kept utilization intentionally low, monitored his reports for accuracy, and left long-standing accounts untouched. He focused on consistency over creativity. He did the boring work, because boring credit is powerful credit.

When it came time to apply for the mortgage, there were no surprises. No last-minute explanations. No scrambling to fix issues under pressure. His approval reflected exactly what his profile had been signaling for months: reliability. That is what strong credit does, it removes chaos from major decisions. It turns life transitions into planned steps instead of stressful events, and it rewards patience with better terms, better pricing, and peace of mind.

Chapter 3 Closing: Understanding Beats Guessing

Credit becomes stressful when people try to manage it emotionally instead of structurally. This chapter was designed to remove that stress by showing you how credit behaves when you understand the rules behind it. Once you stop guessing and start recognizing patterns, your Middle Credit Score stops feeling unpredictable and starts feeling manageable.

You do not need to memorize formulas or monitor your credit obsessively to win. You need consistency, awareness, and the confidence that comes from knowing what matters and what does not. When you understand how balances, timing, and behavior interact, you can make decisions calmly, even when life applies pressure on you.

This chapter was not about doing more. It was about seeing clearly. And clarity is what allows you to move forward without fear, without overcorrecting, and without reacting to every small change. With that understanding in place, you are ready to move from awareness into action, building habits that strengthen your credit over time instead of chasing short-term results.

The One Action Framework

The "Credit Profile Blueprint" Plan (30 / 60 / 90 Days)

Days 1–30: Stabilize and Clean Your File

Pull all three credit reports and mark anything inaccurate, duplicated, outdated, or incomplete. Get current on anything past due (or set up written arrangements), set autopay for minimum payments on every account, and stop new charges on your worst-utilization offenders. The mission in the first 30 days is simple: stop the bleeding, restore order, and regain control.

Days 31–60: Build Momentum with Controlled Behavior

Reduce utilization strategically by targeting the highest-utilization cards first, the ones closest to max, not just the highest interest. Keep older accounts open and active with a small monthly recurring charge and avoid new credit applications while your file is stabilizing. Monitor dispute outcomes and document what moved your Middle Credit Score so you can repeat it.

Days 61–90: Strengthen for Real Opportunities

Push utilization under 30% (toward 10% if you're preparing for a mortgage or refinance) and protect payment history like an asset. Avoid stacking inquiries and keep your profile boring in the best way: accurate reporting, stable balances, clean payments, and no unnecessary new accounts. This is the phase where your file starts looking lender-ready - not just like a "better score.".

Chapter 3 Final Takeaways

- Credit strength is built through repeatable habits, not luck
- Payment history and utilization drive your profile more than most people realize
- Monitoring protects you from errors, fraud, and last-minute surprises
- Short-term fixes matter, but long-term stability is what earns top-tier terms
- A "boring" profile, clean, consistent, and low utilization, is a powerful profile

The Role of Credit During Major Life Transitions

Navigating Credit Through Life's Biggest Changes

Life is full of transitions: buying your first home, starting a family, launching a business, relocating for opportunity, going through a divorce, or preparing for retirement. These are powerful milestones, and they should be moments of pride. However, I've learned over decades of sitting with consumers at the table: transitions do not just change your life; they expose your finances. They put your credit profile under a spotlight, and whether people like it or not, your credit becomes a decision-maker in moments when you want life to move forward quickly.

Over my years as a lender, I have met clients right at the moment they were ready to move forward: first-time homebuyers who worked hard and saved, couples merging households and responsibilities, entrepreneurs with the talent and drive but needing funding, and families simply seeking stability. Again and again, the difference between "approved" and "denied" was not the dream, it was the details: payment history, utilization, derogatory accounts, and errors hiding in plain sight on a report no one reviewed until it was too late.

I wrote this chapter to help you face life's most significant transitions with confidence. During these moments, your Middle Credit Score® and overall credit profile stop being just numbers and become real leverage. With a strong profile, you gain choices, lower costs, and flexibility. With a weak profile, you face friction, delays, and, at times, lingering embarrassment. My goal is both to help you prevent those outcomes and to show you how to recover if you've already experienced them.

Financial setbacks happen. Medical bills, job loss, business slowdowns, divorce, emergencies, and everyday life can all leave marks on your credit report that feel permanent. But hear me clearly: credit challenges are not life sentences. They are events. They are chapters. They are moments that can be corrected and outgrown when you approach credit as a system instead of an emotion.

In this chapter, we will cover the most common credit problems, how they hurt your Middle Credit Score®, and what you can do to reverse the damage. We will look at late payments, high utilization, collections, delinquent accounts, bankruptcy, and the all-too-common errors on credit reports that quietly cost people approvals. Then we will connect it all to major life transitions, so you know how to protect your credit before you need it most. By the end, you will learn how to use credit as a steppingstone, not a stumbling block, during the most significant changes in your life.

Section 1: Common Credit Challenges and Their Impact

Life happens, and sometimes it hits your credit hard. Late payments, high utilization, accounts in collections, charge-offs, and bankruptcies are among the most common challenges I have seen. Each one can feel overwhelming when you're in it, but the first step is recognizing what these issues really are: temporary setbacks that can be managed, repaired, and replaced with better history over time. Your Middle Credit Score® responds to what you do repeatedly, not to what happened once.

Late payments are one of the fastest ways to take a hit, and many people do not understand how the clock works. If you miss a payment by a few days, you might pay a late fee, but it does not always get reported. Once you hit the 30-day mark, it typically shows up as a derogatory mark. When that happens, it is not just a small ding, it can be a meaningful drop that affects approvals, rates, and how lenders view your overall risk.

High credit utilization is another major issue that quietly holds people back. Maxing out cards or carrying high balances signals financial strain, even when you are making minimum payments on time. The credit scoring system does not just reward payment behavior; it also measures how dependent you appear to be on revolving debt. When you are using most of your available credit, the model reads that as overextension, and when lenders see overextension, they assume the next step could be missed payments.

Collections and severe derogatory events, such as bankruptcy, can feel like the end of the road, but they are not. Yes, collections can stay on your report for years, and bankruptcy can remain on your report even longer. But I have seen people rebuild from both. The people who recover the fastest are the ones who stop treating their credit like a mystery and start treating it like a plan. When you address the issue directly, reduce exposure, rebuild positive history, and clean up errors, your score can improve, and your profile can regain credibility.

From My Client Files - Example 19 (Chapter 4): Middle Credit Score® Dropped

---

I have watched this play out in real time. Raquel came to me in a panic after missing two consecutive credit card payments. One late payment had already dropped her Middle Credit Score® by more than 40 points, and she was terrified the next one would ruin her mortgage chances completely. We acted quickly and directly. She called the creditor, explained what happened, negotiated help where possible, and set up automatic payments so it would never happen again. Within a few months, she stabilized, recovered ground, and regained confidence.

From My Client Files - Example 20 (Chapter 4):
Emergency - Credit Cards Maxed

Mike's situation is one I have seen countless times, and it is important because it proves something critical: not all credit damage comes from irresponsibility. Mike never missed a payment. His issue was not behavior, it was circumstance. A sudden emergency forced him to rely on credit cards, and over a short period of time, balances climbed until utilization was maxed out. On paper, the system interpreted that as risk, even though his intent was survival, not overspending.

What made the situation feel worse was the trap that followed. Once balances were high, minimum payments consumed cash flow, progress felt slow, and the score impact lingered. This is where many people give up or start making emotional decisions. Instead, we slowed everything down and focused on structure. We built a payoff sequence that targeted utilization first, not perfection. The goal wasn't to eliminate debt overnight; it was to restore balance and regain control of the ratios lenders measure.

As balances came down, something predictable happened: utilization improved, volatility dropped, and Mike's Middle Credit Score® began to recover. Not all at once, but steadily. There was no trick involved. Just math, discipline, and consistency applied over time. His experience is a reminder that emergencies don't have to permanently define your credit profile. How you respond after the crisis matters more than the crisis itself.

From My Client Files – Example 21 (Chapter 4):
Debt Collections Negotiating

Jessica's situation started the way many do, job loss followed by a missed account that quickly spiraled into collections. What made it overwhelming wasn't just the debt; it was the constant pressure. The calls, the letters, the fear that one mistake had permanently defined her credit. That emotional weight is often more damaging than the account itself, because it causes people to freeze instead of act.

The turning point came when she shifted from avoidance to engagement. We approached the collection strategically. She negotiated directly, demanded clarity, and made sure every agreement was documented in writing before any payment was made. Just as important, she verified that once the account was resolved, it was reported accurately across all bureaus. That step is where many people fail, they settle the debt but never confirm that the credit file reflects the resolution correctly.

What made Jessica's outcome strong wasn't just clearing the collection, it was what she did next. She continued monitoring her reports, protected payment history, and intentionally built new positive credit behavior. Over time, the collection lost its power, and her Middle Credit Score® climbed into the 700s. That result isn't rare. It is what happens when people stop reacting emotionally and start treating credit like a system they can manage.

Section 2: Addressing Errors on Your Credit Report

Mistakes on a credit report are one of the most frustrating parts of personal finance, because you can do everything right and still be penalized for something that is not true. I have seen it repeatedly. Duplicate accounts, wrong balances, misreported late payments, old accounts showing as open, and paid collections still reporting as unpaid. These errors can pull down your Middle Credit Score® and stall approvals at the exact moment you are trying to move forward.

The problem is that most people do not look until they're already in a transaction. They find out there's an issue only when a lender says, "We cannot approve this," and then they scramble. Your credit report is not just a report; it's a financial résumé. If it is wrong, you do not want to learn that on application day. You want to know early enough to fix it and apply from a position of strength.

When you review your reports, be meticulous. Look for anything that changes the story of your credit profile: accounts that are not yours, balances that do not match your statements, on-time payments reported as late, and accounts that should be closed but still show as active. If something is wrong, do not just ignore it, dispute it, and back your dispute with evidence.

From My Client Files – Example 22 (Chapter 4): A Mortgage Denial

---

One of my clients, Toni, came to me after a mortgage denial, feeling confused and frustrated. She paid her bills and genuinely believed she was doing everything right, but her credit report told a different story. It listed a duplicate account with a large, incorrect balance and a late payment on a card she'd closed years earlier. We pulled all three bureau reports, reviewed them line by line, and disputed every inaccurate item with supporting documentation. We also reached out directly to the creditor, because the fastest corrections often come from the source that reported the error.

It required persistence, and these systems rarely move quickly unless you keep the pressure on. But once the corrections went through, her Middle Credit Score® jumped. That improvement did not just lead to approval; it also reduced her interest rate. This is what many people miss: fixing errors isn't only about turning a "no" into a "yes." It's also about lowering the cost of that "yes" over the life of the loan. That's where credit directly impacts wealth.

Section 3: Strategies for Resolving Delinquent Accounts

Delinquent accounts feel heavy because they represent unfinished business, and the longer they sit unresolved, the more damage they can do. But delinquency does not have to define you. What defines you is what you do next. When consumers take action, when they communicate, negotiate, and document their progress they rebuild trust, not just with lenders but with themselves.

If an account is delinquent but still open, the first move is to contact the creditor and work out a plan to bring it current. Most creditors would rather work with you than charge the account off. They want repayment and predictability. If you approach them with a real plan, many will cooperate. If the account is already in collections, you still have options. Settlement is often possible, but it must be handled strategically and in writing. The way it is reported matters because your credit report is a story, and you want the story to show responsibility and resolution.

From My Client Files – Example 23 (Chapter 4): Middle Credit Score® Dropped 200 points

---

James, a small business owner, came to me after a health crisis threw his finances off track. Medical bills piled up, income became unstable, and he leaned on credit to keep life moving. Several accounts fell behind, and one went to collections. His Middle Credit Score dropped from the 700s into the 500s, and he felt stuck. The first thing we did was prioritize the accounts that mattered most, because not all delinquent accounts carry the same weight. We focused on the most significant and most impactful obligations, got payment plans in place, and stabilized the bleeding.

Then we handled the collection account with a settlement plan that he could afford. We ensured everything was documented and tracked, reporting updates. As soon as the accounts started reflecting progress, his profile improved. Within months, his Middle Credit Score began climbing again. That improvement became fuel, and eventually, he was able to request a goodwill adjustment after consistent payments. His recovery wasn't fast because it was a lucky break. It was quick because it was strategic.

Section 4: Rebuilding Credit After Bankruptcy

Bankruptcy is one of the most misunderstood financial tools in America. It carries shame for many people, but what it really represents is a reset when life has become unmanageable. It is not a "get out of responsibility" card. It is a legal structure meant to give people a chance to rebuild. The problem is that many people don't rebuild correctly afterward. They either avoid credit completely out of fear or jump back into debt too quickly without a plan.

Rebuilding after bankruptcy is achievable, but it requires discipline and patience. The system is watching what you do after the event. Over time, positive history begins to outweigh negative history, and the fastest way to build that positive history is through consistent on-time payments and controlled utilization. That is why secured credit cards and credit-builder loans are often powerful first steps. They are not glamorous, but they report positive behavior, and that is what rebuilds a Middle Credit Score.

From My Client Files – Example 24 (Chapter 4):
Chapter 7 Filed, Middle Credit Score Reestablished

Carlos filed for Chapter 7 after medical expenses and job loss created debt he could not recover from. When I met him, his score was in the low 500s, and he felt defeated. But we approached it like a plan, not a punishment. He opened a secured credit card with a small deposit, used it for basic expenses, and paid it off consistently. He set up automatic payments so a late payment would not undo months of progress. He reviewed his credit reports and found errors where discharged accounts were still misreported, and we disputed those items with documentation.

Over time, his profile improved because he stayed consistent. Two years later, his Middle Credit Score was in the high 600s, and he qualified for reasonable financing again. More importantly, he regained confidence. Bankruptcy may stay on a report, but your behavior after bankruptcy becomes the new story lenders trust.

Section 5: Managing High Credit Utilization Is Taking Control of Your Credit Health

High utilization is one of the biggest silent killers of a strong score, and most people do not realize how much it matters until they apply for something important. You can pay every bill on time and still struggle to qualify if your credit cards are near their max limits. That is because utilization tells the scoring model a straightforward thing: how dependent you appear to be on revolving credit. The higher your dependence, the higher your perceived risk.

The fastest way to improve utilization is to pay down balances, especially on high-interest cards. But there are also strategic moves that can help if you are disciplined. One is requesting a credit limit increase, which lowers your utilization ratio without paying off a dollar if, and only if, you do not use the extra credit. Another strategy is to distribute your balances, so you do not max out one card. In contrast, others sit unused because the optics of a single maxed-out account can hurt you even if your overall utilization looks acceptable.

The important thing here is mindset. When you're working to improve your Middle Credit Score, you are not playing a game for points. You are building a profile that lenders trust. Lower utilization is one of the most direct ways to do that. It is proof that you can access credit without being consumed by it.

Section 6: Protecting Your Credit During Financial Hardships

Hardship is where credit is most damaged, not because people are irresponsible, but because stress distorts decision-making. Job loss, medical emergencies, divorce, business slowdowns; these moments create urgency, which leads to panic spending, missed payments, and silence. Silence is where the real damage happens, because creditors and lenders cannot help you if you disappear.

If you know a hardship is coming, communicate early. Many creditors offer hardship programs, temporary reduced payments, or deferrals that can help you avoid late reporting. The key is to ask before you are behind. At the same time, you must prioritize the essentials. Keeping your housing and transportation stable matters, and secured obligations often carry bigger consequences if they fall behind.

From My Client Files - Example 25 (Chapter 4): Small Business Owner

---

Andy, a small business owner, faced a medical emergency that drained his savings and reduced his income. He feared late payments would destroy his credit and make recovery even more complicated. Instead of waiting, he contacted his mortgage lender and credit card issuers early. He secured a short-term deferral and temporarily reduced his minimum payments, which helped him maintain good standing while he stabilized. He also monitored his reports and caught an error, a duplicate late payment entry that he disputed and removed.

Six months later, he had stabilized his finances and protected his Middle Credit Score through the storm's most challenging part. The takeaway is simple: hardships do not destroy credit on their own. The absence of a plan does.

Section 7: Establishing a Plan for Long-Term Credit Recovery

Recovering from credit challenges is not just about fixing what went wrong, it is about creating a structure that prevents repeat damage. Most consumers can recover credit, but those who stay strong build a system. They automate payments. They track balances. They reduce utilization intentionally. They check reports regularly, and set clear goals, so progress becomes measurable rather than emotional.

Long-term recovery is built on consistency. That means on-time payments every month, not just when you feel like it. It means keeping your spending under control, even when life tempts you to spend. It means monitoring reports to catch errors early. It means rebuilding with intention, not with random new credit lines that create more risk than benefit.

From My Client Files - Example 26 (Chapter 4): Job Loss – High Credit Card Use

I worked with a client, Megan who experienced a chain reaction of setbacks which included job loss, reliance on credit cards, utilization spiking, and then missed payments. Her Middle Credit Score dropped sharply, and she believed there was no way back. But recovery is always possible with a plan. We negotiated where needed, built a payoff strategy, added controlled positive reporting, and monitored her reports for errors. Over time, she climbed back into strong territory, qualified again, and regained financial stability. The lesson is this: credit recovery is not a one-step process. It is a pattern.

Section 8: The Importance of Credit Counseling

Sometimes the problem isn't a lack of effort. Sometimes it's overwhelmed. When people are drowning in bills, creditor calls, and stress, they don't need motivation, they need structure. That is where nonprofit credit counseling can help. A reputable counselor can guide you toward a manageable plan, sometimes negotiating interest rates and fees, while also allowing you to build a realistic budget and stronger financial habits.

Credit counseling isn't about embarrassment. It is about support. It is about getting a plan that matches your income and your life. The wrong move is turning to predatory settlement companies that promise miracles and sometimes make the situation worse.

The right move is working with a reputable organization that focuses on stability and education, not shortcuts.

I have seen clients regain control through counseling because it gave them one thing they did not have: a clear path. When the path is clear, action becomes easier. When action becomes easier, consistency follows, and consistency is what improves your Middle Credit Score over time.

Section 9: Credit During Major Life Transitions

The 90-Day Rule I Used as a Lender

Here is what most people do not understand until it is too late: major life transitions do not just require money, they require timing, and credit is deeply tied to timing. People get denied not because their dream is wrong, but because they make preventable credit moves at the worst possible moment. That's why I always taught a simple rule when I was guiding consumers through approvals.

The rule is this: ninety days before a significant transition, protect your credit like it is your job. In the ninety days before you apply for a mortgage, sign a lease, finance a vehicle, or pursue a primary approval, you must be careful. You do not open new accounts casually. You do not spike balances. You do not co-sign. You do not finance furniture. You do not make emotional purchases "because we're excited." You keep things calm, controlled, and predictable.

I have watched deals collapse over one store credit card. I have watched approvals disappear because someone charged a large balance right before closing. I have watched a consumer's middle score drop because they maxed out a card to buy appliances, not realizing that utilization updates could hit at the worst time. Credit is not just a score; it's a snapshot, and you want that snapshot to show stability when the lender takes it.

Major life transitions trigger **credit exposure**:

- Buying a home
- Renting
- Relocating
- Marriage / Divorce
- Starting a business
- Retirement

In these moments, you do not need random advice. You need a rule:

The 90-Day Rule

Ninety days before any major transition, protect your credit like it's your job.

Most people do not get denied because their credit is "terrible." They get dismissed because they make preventable moves at the worst time.

In the 90 days before a mortgage or primary approval:

- Don't open new accounts
- Don't finance furniture
- Don't co-sign
- Don't spike balances
- Don't miss payments
- Don't ignore your reports

I have seen deals collapse over a store card, a maxed-out balance, or a single missed payment that could have been avoided with a reminder.

Credit is not just a score. Credit is timing.

Chapter 4 Closing: Credit Is a Transition Tool

If there's one thing I have learned over three decades of sitting with consumers during life's most significant moments, it is this: transitions do not just change your life, they expose your finances. Homeownership, divorce, relocation, starting a business, expanding a family, retirement… these are not just emotional decisions. They are underwriting decisions too, and the difference between "we are moving forward" and "we have to wait" is often your Middle Credit Score and the condition of your overall credit file.

Credit challenges are not life sentences. They are events. They are chapters, and they can be corrected and outgrown when you treat credit like a system, not an emotion. Late payments can be stabilized. Utilization can be reduced. Errors can be removed.

Collections can be resolved strategically. Bankruptcy can become a reset that leads to a stronger profile than the one you had before. The people who win are not the ones who never get hit. They are the ones who respond with a plan.

Here is the rule I want you to carry into every significant life move, **credit is timing.** Ninety days before a transition, protect your credit like it is your job, because most people do not get denied because their credit is "terrible." They get dismissed because they make preventable moves at the worst time.

The One Action Framework

The "90-Day Transition Protection" Plan (30 / 60 / 90 Days)

Days 1–30: Stabilize and Stop the Damage

Pull all three reports and identify what's hurting your Middle Credit Score the most: late payments, high utilization, collections, reporting errors, or delinquent accounts. Get current on any past-due items (or set written arrangements), contact creditors early if hardship is present, and dispute inaccuracies immediately with documentation. The first 30 days are about control: stop the bleeding and prevent further damage.

Days 31–60: Resolve, Reduce, and Rebuild

Strategically lower utilization by targeting the highest-utilization cards first and keeping balances under control. Resolve collections or delinquent accounts with a written plan and make sure reporting updates are correct after resolution. If you are rebuilding after a major event (including bankruptcy), start with controlled, positive reporting using a secured card or a credit-builder approach, and keep it boring and consistent.

Days 61–90: Protect the Snapshot Before the Transition
This is where approvals are won or lost, no new accounts. No co-signing. No financing furniture. No balance spikes. No "celebration spending" that turns into higher utilization. Keep your payment history flawless, keep utilization trending down (toward 10% if possible), verify your reports are accurate across all three bureaus, and make your profile calm, stable, and lender ready. Because **credit is not just a score, it's timing.**

Chapter 4 Final Takeaways

- Major life transitions expose your credit, so preparation beats panic
- Credit challenges aren't permanent, because organized action replaces negative history over time
- Errors must be disputed early; timing determines whether you pay more or qualify sooner
- Utilization is a silent score killer, even when you pay on time
- Delinquencies and collections can be resolved, but reporting accuracy is everything
- Bankruptcy is a reset: rebuilding works when behavior becomes consistent
- The **90-day window** before a significant move is sacred: protect the snapshot

The Role of the Major Credit Bureaus

The Backbone of Credit Reporting

Credit reporting is the engine that quietly runs the modern financial system, and at its center are the three major credit bureaus: Experian, Equifax, and TransUnion. Most people don't think about these bureaus until they are applying for something important like a mortgage, a car, an apartment, or a major credit card. Whether you're paying attention or not, the bureaus are recording the story of your financial behavior and distributing that story to the companies deciding what you qualify for, how much it will cost, and how quickly you can move forward.

Over the years, I have watched consumers walk into life-changing moments thinking they were "fine," only to find out their credit profile was working against them. Sometimes it was their utilization. Sometimes it was a late payment they forgot about. Sometimes it was a collection they did not know existed. More often than people realize, it was simply wrong information. A reporting error, a duplicate account, an outdated balance, or an account that should have been marked paid but was not. Those mistakes do not just hurt feelings. They change approvals. They change rates. They change the total cost of a loan over the next 15 or 30 years.

As a lender, I learned quickly that the bureaus are not just "part of the process." They are the foundation on which the process is built. The credit report is what underwriters pull because they need to decide, and that report is only as good as the data inside it. The bureaus do not wake up trying to hurt consumers, but they also do not live in your house. They do not know your life. They do not know what you intended. They only know what gets reported, how it gets coded, and whether the supporting documentation matches when a dispute is filed. That is why knowledge matters. When you understand how the bureaus operate, you stop being a bystander in your own financial future.

Another misconception I have seen repeatedly is the belief that the credit bureaus make the decisions. They are not. Experian, Equifax, and TransUnion do not approve or deny your loan. They do not set your interest rate. They do not decide if you can rent that apartment or get that job. What they do is supply the report and the data on which decisions are made. They provide the raw material. Lenders and scoring models convert that raw material into risk.

This is where your Middle Credit Score® becomes the centerpiece. Most mortgage lending decisions are made using the middle of your three scores, one score from each bureau's dataset. That means you do not need perfection across all three, but you do need accuracy across all three. One incorrect entry can lower your Middle Credit Score®. Having one outdated bureau can move you to a different pricing tier. One bureau with a missing positive history can cost you the best terms, even if the other two look great. When you understand this, you start treating your credit reports like what they really are: the most essential financial file you own.

This chapter is designed to pull back the curtain. We are going to go bureau by bureau and get practical. You will learn what the bureaus do, why your reports differ, how their tools can help you, and how to use monitoring and disputes to keep your credit profile aligned with reality. By the end of this chapter, you will understand how to navigate the credit reporting system with confidence, and how to protect your Middle Credit Score so it reflects your true financial potential.

Section 1: What Are Credit Bureaus and What Do They Actually Do?

Credit bureaus, also called credit reporting agencies, collect organize, and distribute credit-related information about consumers. They are not banks, lenders, or the government. They are data companies. Their entire business model is built around collecting information from creditors and public sources, then packaging it into reports for evaluating risk.

When you borrow money, open a credit card, finance a car, or even have an account sent to collections, the activity around those accounts can be reported to the bureaus. Over time, the bureaus compile a profile that includes your payment history, balances, limits, account age, credit mix, and inquiries that indicate when you have applied for credit. That profile becomes your credit report, and your credit report becomes the foundation for most scoring models.

One thing I want to make clear is this: the bureaus do not "decide" your score; they control the data that produces it. Think of it like this. If your credit score is the final grade, your credit report is the test. And if the test has wrong answers printed on it, your grade will be bad too. That is why understanding the bureaus matters. If you want to protect your Middle Credit Score, you must ensure the accuracy and completeness of the reports that feed it.

Credit bureaus also serve a broader purpose in the financial system. They create a standardized way for lenders to evaluate borrowers at scale. Without credit reporting, every lender would have to verify and assess risk from scratch. With credit reporting, lenders can make decisions quickly. That speed creates convenience for consumers, but it also creates a system where errors, omissions, and inconsistent reporting can cause real damage if you aren't actively monitoring your file.

And the final reality is that credit bureaus are not only used by mortgage lenders. Landlords may check credit. Insurance companies may use credit-based information in pricing in certain states. Some employers may review certain credit information in regulated ways for specific roles. That is why this is bigger than loans. Your credit report has become a modern financial identity document.

Section 2: The Big Three: Experian, Equifax, and TransUnion

Experian, Equifax, and TransUnion all perform the same core function: they collect data, compile it into a report, and distribute it to authorized users. But they are not identical. They do not receive the same information at the same time, from the same sources, in the same format. That is one of the most essential realities consumers need to understand, because it explains why your three reports can look like three different versions of your financial life.

Experian is widely known for its consumer-facing tools and its efforts to incorporate additional positive data into reports. It also has a large footprint in the credit ecosystem, and lenders often pull Experian data because of its scale and availability. For many consumers, Experian is the bureau where they first interact with credit management tools, and it is often the first place they learn what is really in their report.

Equifax has long been a key player in the credit system, and it has also developed deep relationships in employment and income verification through its Workforce Solutions operations. While that is not the same as credit reporting, it matters because employment verification and credit reporting often intersect in underwriting and risk evaluation. Equifax also serves as a significant repository of credit information, and like the other bureaus, its report becomes part of the data used to produce a score.

TransUnion is often associated with 'trended data'—models that look at how balances and payments move over time, not just a single monthly snapshot. Instead of viewing your credit use as a single snapshot, trended approaches look at whether your balances are rising or falling and how consistently you manage revolving accounts over a period. Even when you are doing the right things today, your historical trends can influence how risk is perceived, depending on the scoring model and lending context.

What matters most is this: when lenders use the middle score method, the three bureaus are not optional. They become a system. If one bureau has an error, the middle score can be skewed. If one bureau is missing a positive account, your middle score can be lower than it should be. If one bureau shows an outdated delinquency, it can be the deciding factor that pushes your middle credit score below a key threshold.

I saw this firsthand with a client who was denied despite appearing to have strong credit behavior. We pulled his reports and found that TransUnion still showed a paid delinquency as active. That single issue pulled his TransUnion score down, and because the lender used the middle score, it lowered his pricing tier. The solution wasn't complicated, but it required knowledge and urgency. We disputed it with documentation, verified that the other two reports were accurate, and the correction restored his middle credit score to a range that qualified him for better terms. The lesson was not that the system is unfair. The lesson was that the system must be managed.

Section 3: Why Credit Reports Differ Across Bureaus

One of the most common questions consumers ask is, "Why are my scores different?" The answer is simple, but essential: your scores differ because your reports differ, and your reports differ because your data is not perfectly uniform across all three bureaus.

The first reason is reporting coverage. Not every creditor reports to all three bureaus. Some creditors report to only one or two. Sometimes, smaller lenders choose limited reporting to reduce costs. Sometimes the reporting relationship changes over time. Sometimes, a collection agency reports to one bureau aggressively and to another bureau inconsistently. This creates gaps. And those gaps can make one bureau's report look "thinner" or "worse" than another.

The second reason is timing. Creditors typically update account information monthly, but the timing of those updates is not perfectly synchronized. One bureau may process an update quickly, while another bureau lags. That can temporarily make balances appear different, payment statuses appear inconsistent or cause closed accounts to remain open longer than they should. If you are applying for credit during one of these timing gaps, your score can reflect "yesterday's reality" instead of today's.

The third reason is errors and omissions. Duplicate accounts happen. Old collections appear even after they have been resolved. Closed accounts sometimes report incorrectly. Late payments can be misreported. Positive accounts can be missing, and what makes this especially frustrating is that the error may appear on only one bureau. That means you can pull two reports with confidence, only to get blindsided by the third.

The fourth reason is the scoring model and the dataset used. Even when the underlying factors are similar, the way models interpret, and weigh details can vary. On the mortgage side, the scoring versions used are often different than what consumers see in general credit monitoring apps. That creates confusion because people assume the score they see, is the score the lender sees. Sometimes it is close. Sometimes it is not. This is why I consistently tell consumers to focus less on the app score and more on report accuracy and the middle credit score method.

From My Client Files - Example 27 (Chapter 5): Equifax, TransUnion and Experian All Contained Different Information

I had a client, Tammy who thought her middle score was "wrong" because she had strong habits. However, her Equifax report still showed an old balance that had already been paid down. Experian showed the correct low balance. TransUnion didn't show the account at all. So, the lender's middle credit score did not reflect her real behavior, it reflected inconsistent reporting. Once we corrected the Equifax data and ensured the creditor reported consistently, her middle credit score rebounded, and the pricing improved. This is precisely why monitoring all three bureaus is necessary. Your middle credit score is only as reliable as the least accurate bureau.

Section 4: Monitoring Your Credit Reports

Monitoring your credit reports is not paranoia. It is maintenance. It is like checking the oil in your car before the engine fails. Most credit disasters do not happen because a consumer is careless. They occur because no one looked until a lender looked, and by then, the consumer is reacting under pressure.

When you monitor your reports, you are doing more than searching for fraud. You are checking your financial story for accuracy. You are verifying that your balances are reporting correctly, that closed accounts are marked closed, that paid collections reflect paid status where appropriate, and that no unfamiliar accounts or inquiries appear. You are also checking that your positive accounts, your long-standing credit lines and strong payment histories are being reported in full. Missing positive history can hurt just as much as a negative mark.

The most important thing I want consumers to understand is that monitoring protects the middle. Because the middle credit score method depends on all three bureaus, you do not get to ignore one report just because the other two look fine. If you do, the one report you ignored can become the one score that changes your outcome.

From My Client Files - Example 28 (Chapter 5):
Unable to Refinance

Sandee, a client, once came to me with a sudden drop that prevented her from refinancing. She had done nothing reckless. Errors caused the drop: one bureau showed a paid medical bill as unpaid, another showed a balance on a closed card, and the third bureau omitted a positive account that would have strengthened the middle. None of this was "her fault," but it was her responsibility to correct once it was discovered. We filed disputes with documentation, contacted the creditor for consistent reporting, and then put monitoring in place so she would not be surprised again. Within weeks, her middle score recovered, and she refinanced on better terms. That is the power of staying ahead of the file.

Monitoring also gives you a timing advantage. When you catch an issue early, you can resolve it before you apply for something significant. When you see it late, you're trying to repair a profile while an underwriter is waiting on conditions. That pressure creates rushed decisions and missed opportunities. The goal is not just to have good credit. The goal is to have a clean, accurate report when it matters most.

Section 5: The Impact of Data Accuracy on Your Middle Credit Score

Your Middle Credit Score is not an opinion. It is a calculation. And the calculation is only as correct as the data feeding it. That's why accuracy is everything. A single misreported late payment can dramatically lower a score. An inflated balance can raise your utilization and reduce your score even if you are active in managing your credit responsibly. A missing positive account can shrink the depth of your file and lower your score because the model sees less proof of stability.

In lending, minor differences can lead to significant outcomes. I have seen consumers miss the best mortgage pricing tier by a few points. I have seen rate adjustments triggered by a score threshold. I have seen approvals delayed because an account that should have been closed was still showing open with a balance. What makes those situations painful is that many of them are preventable with early review and correction.

Accuracy also matters because lenders don't always have the flexibility to "ignore" what's on the report, even when the consumer has a reasonable explanation. Underwriting is built on documentation. If the report indicates something is delinquent, the lender must treat it as delinquent until it is corrected or documented in compliance with applicable requirements. That means the fastest path is not arguing emotionally with the system. The quickest route is correcting the data.

From My Client Files - Example 29 (Chapter 5): One Late Payment

I worked with a client, Maurice, whose middle score was being dragged down by a single late payment that was incorrectly reported. He had proof of on-time payments, but the bureau report told a different story. Once we disputed it and the bureau corrected it, his score rose enough to meaningfully change his loan pricing. That is what I mean when I say accuracy is money. A corrected report can literally be worth thousands over time.

While accuracy is not only about mistakes, it is also about protection. Identity theft is a growing issue, and when fraudulent accounts appear, they do not just harm your score, they create a mess that can take time to untangle. Early detection through monitoring and regular review is one of your strongest defenses. You protect your middle credit score by protecting your data.

Section 6: Tools and Resources Provided by the Bureaus

The credit bureaus do not just sell reports to lenders. They also provide tools to consumers, and when those tools are used correctly, they can help you manage, protect, and sometimes improve your credit profile. The problem is that many consumers either do not know these tools exist or do not understand what they do.

Some tools focus on visibility. They help you see your file, track changes, and understand how activity affects your score over time. Other tools focus on protection, such as locking access to your report to reduce the risk of unauthorized activity. Some tools focus on adding positive data that traditional reporting may not capture, which can help consumers with thin files or limited conventional credit history.

Experian, for example, has introduced consumer tools that allow certain on-time payments like utilities and certain subscriptions to be included in a consumer-facing credit dataset. For some people, this can create a meaningful improvement because it provides evidence of reliability that was not previously counted. For others, it will not change much. But the bigger point is that the bureau tools represent leverage. They give you ways to interact with your file, rather than leaving you powerless.

Equifax and TransUnion also offer monitoring and protection tools that can alert you when something changes. Alerts matter because speed matters. If you learn about a new inquiry or account the day it appears, you can act immediately. If you know about it three months later, you are now repairing history instead of preventing damage.

From My Client Files - Example 30 (Chapter 5): A Misreported Account

---

I worked with Ivan who was preparing for a significant mortgage application and had no idea what his reports even looked like. We pulled all three reports, identified an account that was misreported as delinquent, monitored the correction process, added legitimate positive payment data where possible, and protected the file from unnecessary inquiries while the mortgage process was underway. The result was a stronger middle score, better terms, and a smoother path to closing. That is the real purpose of bureau tools: not gimmicks, but control.

The most important thing I want you to take away from this section is that tools only help when they are paired with discipline. A monitoring app will not improve your score if your balances stay maxed out. A lock will not improve your score if the report is inaccurate. A boosted dataset will not help if you still have unresolved derogatory accounts. But when tools are used as part of a strategy, they become powerful. They allow you to protect your middle credit score and keep your financial story accurate.

Section 7: Navigating Disputes with the Credit Bureaus

Errors on credit reports can feel like a brick wall, especially when you discover them right before a significant life move such as buying a home, refinancing, leasing an apartment, or even applying for a job that requires a background review. Over the years, I have sat with clients who felt embarrassed, angry, and confused because their credit reports told a story they did not recognize. The truth is, inaccurate reporting is more common than people think, and it can happen to anyone. A paid account can still show unpaid. A balance can be reported higher than it truly is. A late payment can be applied to the wrong month. Even something as simple as a mixed file where information from another person ends up on your report can disrupt your entire financial plan.

The dispute process is how you correct that story, and it is not about luck. It is about preparation, precision, and persistence. The credit bureaus are required to investigate disputes under the Fair Credit Reporting Act (FCRA), but they can only evaluate what they can verify. That means your dispute must be clear and supported by documentation. When disputes fail, it is often not because the consumer was wrong, it is because the consumer didn't provide enough proof, did not describe the issue clearly, or did not follow through when the bureau responded with a generic or incomplete result.

I always remind people: the bureau is not your enemy, but it is not your advocate either. It is a system, and systems respond best to clean input. A substantial dispute includes the exact account, the exact error, the exact correction requested, and the documents that prove why that correction should be made. Your goal is to make it easier for the bureau to correct the file than to keep it as-is. When you do that, the process becomes much more predictable.

I have seen disputes change outcomes fast. I have seen clients go from denial to approval simply by removing one incorrect late payment or correcting one inflated balance. I have also seen the opposite, where someone who had time to fix an issue but waited too long, then got forced into a higher interest rate because the correction did not come through in time. When it comes to protecting your Middle Credit Score, timing matters. You want your file clean before underwriting begins, not while an underwriter is looking at it.

Disputes also require strategy. Not every negative item is a dispute item. If the account is accurate but unfavorable, your plan may involve negotiation, settlement documentation, goodwill requests, or rebuilding not disputing. However, if it is inaccurate, incomplete, outdated, duplicated, or unverifiable, you absolutely should dispute it. Your credit report is a financial identity document, and you have the right to make sure it is correct.

From My Client Files - Example 31 (Chapter 5): Denied Auto Loan

---

One of my clients, William, was denied an auto loan because of a collection that had already been paid years earlier. It was not even showing across all three bureaus, just one. But because lenders often look at the complete profile, and your middle credit score method relies on three datasets, that one error created a chain reaction. We gathered the proof, submitted the dispute with clean documentation, and followed up until it was removed. Within one bureau cycle, the issue was gone, the score increased, and the approval terms improved. That is why I say disputes are not paperwork, they are leverage.

---

5 Actionable Steps for Navigating Disputes with the Credit Bureaus

1. **Identify the Exact Error Clearly**
   Carefully review your credit reports line by line and pinpoint the specific item you believe is wrong. Write down the bureau reporting it, the creditor name, the account number (partial is fine), and precisely what is inaccurate. Your dispute must focus on one clear issue at a time to avoid confusion and delay.

2. **Gather Supporting Documentation Before You File**
   Collect proof that directly supports your claim. This might include bank statements, receipts, account statements, payoff letters, settlement confirmations, emails from a creditor, or screenshots from an account portal. The more precise and organized your evidence, the stronger your case becomes.

3. **File the Dispute with the Correct Bureau**
   Submit your dispute to the bureau that is reporting the error. You can dispute online or by mail, but your explanation should be concise and specific regardless of the method. State what is wrong, what the correct information should be, and include your documentation to support the correction.

4. **Follow Up and Track the Timeline**
   Bureaus generally have 30 days to investigate. Mark your calendar, track your submission date, and monitor for updates. If the bureau responds without truly addressing

the issue, do not assume it is over, respond again with added documentation and a more explicit request.

5. **Verify the Correction and Protect the Improvement**
Once the bureau updates your file, pull the updated report and confirm the correction is reflected. If the same error reappears later, you may need to dispute again, along with addressing the source, meaning the creditor or collection agency that keeps misreporting it.

Section 8: The Future of Credit Reporting

Credit reporting is changing, and the next decade will look very different from the last 30 years. For a long time, creditworthiness was measured through a narrow lens such as credit cards, installment loans, and a handful of traditional reporting categories. That model worked for some people, but it left millions of responsible adults invisible. They paid rent and utilities on time for years, kept their household running, and still could not qualify for good lending terms because the system did not count the payments that proved their stability.

Now, the credit industry is slowly shifting toward a more complete view of financial behavior. Alternative data is becoming more mainstream, and while it is not perfect, it's a significant step toward fairness for consumers with limited traditional credit history. Rent, utilities, and certain subscription payments, things that reflect real-world responsibility are increasingly being recognized as meaningful. That shift can help consumers build a stronger file without taking on unnecessary debt just to "create credit."

At the same time, technology is pushing credit reporting into a faster, more dynamic era. Artificial intelligence and machine learning are being used to detect patterns, assess risk more precisely, and potentially reduce the impact of isolated mistakes. Instead of viewing your credit report as a static snapshot, the future is leaning toward understanding your behavior over time, how consistently you pay, whether your balances are rising or falling, and how stable your financial habits are month to month and year to year.

Another significant change is consumer control. More tools now let you lock your report, monitor changes in real time, and respond quickly if fraud or errors occur. This is critical because identity theft and data breaches are part of modern life. Your credit profile is valuable, and bad actors know it. The future of credit reporting will increasingly involve proactive protection, not reactive repair.

There is also a growing conversation about transparency and accountability. Consumers are demanding more precise explanations when data affects outcomes, and regulators continue to scrutinize how credit information is collected, reported, and corrected. That matters because the credit system isn't just a private industry anymore, it is a gatekeeper for housing, transportation, insurance, and opportunity. The bureaus will continue to evolve, but consumers who stay informed will always have an advantage.

From My Client Files - Example 32 (Chapter 5): Alternate Reporting Data

---

I worked with a client, Allen, who did not fit the traditional credit mold. He was not reckless. He was not late. He simply had not used credit in the way the system historically rewarded. What he did have was years of perfect rent payments, on-time utility bills, and consistent monthly obligations that showed responsibility and stability. But none of that was visible in his traditional credit file. To the system, he looked thin. To a lender, that often translates to uncertainty.

Once we reviewed his situation, the strategy became clear: if the system evaluates what it can see, then the goal is to make sure the right information is visible. Using legitimate bureau-supported tools, we added verified alternative data to his profile that included rent, and utility history that accurately reflected his real-world behavior. This was not about inflating a score or forcing an outcome. It was about correcting an incomplete picture.

As that data began reporting, something important happened. His credit profile gained depth. His Middle Credit Score did not jump overnight, but it improved enough to move him into a better pricing tier. That shift mattered. It meant lower borrowing costs, more favorable terms, and access that simply was not there before. The system did not suddenly become generous, it became informed.

That experience reinforced something I have seen repeatedly over the years: the credit system is evolving. It's slowly recognizing behavior beyond just credit cards and loans. But the people who benefit from that evolution will not be the ones who ignore it or assume it "doesn't apply to them." The winners will be the ones who understand how reporting works, monitor what's being captured, and use available tools strategically. Credit does not reward intention. It rewards documented behavior, and when the right behavior is visible, the system responds.

---

5 Actionable Steps to Prepare for the Future of Credit Reporting

1. **Use Alternative Data When It Helps Your Profile**
   If you have limited credit history or want additional positive depth, explore legitimate options that allow rent or utility payments to be reflected where applicable. The goal is to strengthen your file with real behavior, not manufactured debt.

2. **Make Credit Monitoring a Normal Habit, not a Panic Move**
   The future will move faster, and your credit changes, good or bad, will reflect quicker. Monitoring helps you catch issues early, respond to fraud immediately, and keep your Middle Credit Score protected before major applications.

3. **Understand That "Your Score" Depends on the Model Being Used**
   As new scoring models evolve, you will continue to see differences between what you see in apps and what lenders use. Focus on the health of your report and the fundamentals of payment history, utilization, age, and accuracy, as these remain the foundation across models.

4. **Use Credit Locks and Security Tools Proactively**
   If you are not applying for credit, consider tools that reduce the risk of unauthorized inquiries. Protection does

not raise your score, but it prevents damage that can take months to undo.

5. **Stay Educated and Adjust Your Strategy as the System Evolves**
   As reporting expands and tools improve, keep learning. A consumer who understands the rules always has more control than a consumer who doesn't.

Additional Client Examples (Chapter 5)

From My Client Files - Example 33 (Chapter 5): Credit Utilization Puzzle

---

Lisa was preparing to apply for a mortgage and felt confident about her credit profile, but her middle credit score came back lower than projected. After reviewing her reports, she discovered one credit card had reported right after a large purchase, even though she paid it down shortly after. That single reporting cycle pushed utilization higher and pulled down the bureau score used in the middle calculation. We timed a mid-cycle payment and waited for the balance to update. Once it did, her middle score moved into a stronger pricing tier. That adjustment didn't just raise a score; it reduced risk perception, improved terms, and lowered the long-term cost of financing.

From My Client Files - Example 34 (Chapter 5): Qualified for a Lower Interest Rate

---

Josh had a solid credit foundation but knew he was paying more than necessary on a personal loan. His payment history was clean, but several accounts showed higher reported balances than he realized because of statement timing. We focused on adjusting when payments were made so lower balances were reported, not changing how much he spent. Once those updates reflected across his reports, his score improved enough to qualify for a noticeably lower interest rate. Nothing about his discipline changed; the difference was aligning his behavior with how the system measures risk.

What stood out to Josh afterward was how narrow the gap had been. He wasn't missing payments, overusing credit, or making mistakes. He simply hadn't understood how reporting mechanics shaped outcomes. Once he did, credit stopped feeling unpredictable. The lower rate saved him money immediately, but the bigger shift was confidence. Josh no longer viewed credit as something that "happened" to him. He learned how small adjustments, made intentionally, could unlock better terms and long-term efficiency without changing his lifestyle.

From My Client Files- Example 35 (Chapter 5): Lenders use the Middle Credit Score®

Emma assumed all three credit bureaus were telling the same story. Like most consumers, she believed that if one report looked accurate, the others probably did too. But when she took the time to review all three, she noticed something subtle but important: TransUnion was reporting a higher balance on one of her revolving accounts than what was owed. It was not a dramatic error, and at first glance it did not feel urgent. But that single discrepancy increased her utilization on that bureau just enough to suppress the score tied to it.

What Emma did not realize at first was that this was not just "one bureau being off", because lenders often rely on the Middle Credit Score®, that inflated balance did not stay isolated. It directly affected the score that underwriting would trust most. In other words, the bureau with the error became the one that quietly controlled her loan pricing. Once she understood that, her mindset shifted from casual monitoring to strategic action.

She gathered her statements, submitted a clean dispute with documentation, and followed up until the correction posted. When the balance updated correctly, the reports aligned, utilization normalized, and her Middle Credit Score rose. Nothing about Emma's financial behavior changed. What changed was accuracy, and that accuracy removed an invisible penalty she had been paying without realizing it.

The lesson here is one I've seen repeat countless times: small reporting errors can create outsized consequences when they hit the bureau that controls the middle credit score. Emma didn't win because she chased a higher number. She won because she protected the number that mattered.

From My Client Files - Example 36 (Chapter 5): Suspicious Credit Inquiry

Michael didn't discover the problem because his score dropped; he caught it because he was paying attention. While reviewing his credit activity, he noticed an inquiry he did not recognize. On its own, a single inquiry might seem minor. But Michael understood something most consumers do not: unauthorized inquiries are often the first visible sign of attempted fraud, not the last. Waiting would have allowed the situation to escalate.

Instead of freezing or assuming it would "work itself out," he acted immediately. He contacted the bureau, disputed the inquiry through the proper channels, and activated protective tools to limit further exposure. He also placed additional safeguards on his credit file so no new accounts could be opened without verification. Speed mattered. The faster he responded, the smaller the footprint the fraud attempt left behind.

The real win was not just removing the inquiry; it was what Michael learned. He shifted from passive monitoring to proactive protection. He understood how inquiries appear, how bureaus handle disputes, and how to lock down access before real damage occurs. That knowledge turned a potential problem into a long-term advantage. Credit security is not about reacting after harm is done; it's about knowing how to stop problems before they spread.

From My Client Files - Example 37 (Chapter 5): Didn't Wait for Underwriting, She Pulled All 3 Credit Reports

---

Laura knew a mortgage application was coming, and instead of assuming her credit was "fine," she chose to verify it early. She pulled all three credit reports and reviewed them line by line. In the process, she spotted an account reporting as open with a balance that should have been closed and paid. Left uncorrected, it would have inflated her utilization and raised questions in underwriting. She disputed the error immediately, followed through with documentation, and had the item corrected before any lender ever accessed her file.

What separated Laura's experience from most borrowers was control. She did not wait for a lender to uncover the issue and frame the conversation. By acting early, she eliminated surprises, avoided processing delays, and protected her pricing. When underwriting reviewed her file, it told a clean, stable story with no interruptions. That is the power of early review: corrections happen calmly, approvals move smoothly, and leverage stays with the borrower instead of shifting to the clock.

Chapter 5 Closing: Your Credit Reports Are Your Financial File

Let me be clear about something most people learn too late: your credit score does not exist on its own. It's built from data, the data that lives inside three separate reports, updated at different times, by various systems, with varying margins for error. When that data is wrong, incomplete, or ignored, the outcomes are not just inconvenient, they are expensive. I've seen borrowers with substantial income and good intentions pay more simply because one bureau told a different story.

This chapter was not about creating fear or encouraging obsession. It was about awareness. When you understand how Experian, Equifax, and TransUnion operate, you stop reacting to surprises and start managing your financial file intentionally. You no longer hope your best score shows up; you ensure your entire profile is accurate, calm, and lender ready.

Your Middle Credit Score® is not a mystery once you treat your reports like what they truly are: a financial record that deserves the same attention as your bank accounts or tax returns. When you manage that record proactively, you walk into approvals with leverage instead of questions. That is not luck. That's preparation.

The One Action Framework

The "Clean File Advantage" Plan (30 / 60 / 90 Days)

Days 1–30: See the Truth and Identify the Damage

Pull all three bureau reports and compare them line by line. Highlight anything inaccurate, duplicated, outdated, or missing. Identify which bureau is hurting your Middle Credit Score the most and why (utilization, late payment, collection reporting, missing account, incorrect status). Set your baseline: your three scores and your actual middle score.

Days 31–60: Correct the Data and Stabilize the Profile

File disputes on inaccurate items with clean documentation and one explicit request per dispute. Follow up until the bureau updates correctly. At the same time, stabilize the behaviors that move scores: protect payment history, strategically reduce utilization, and avoid unnecessary inquiries. If you're not actively applying for credit, consider protecting your reports with the right security tools to prevent new damage while the corrections process is underway.

Days 61–90: Align the Reports and Protect the Snapshot

Verify that corrections are posted correctly across all three bureaus, not just one. Confirm balances, statuses, and closed/paid reporting are accurate. Make your profile calm and predictable: low utilization, no new accounts, no random inquiries, no last-minute financial moves. This is how you protect your Middle Credit Score before it matters and walk into any primary approval with leverage not surprises.

Chapter 5 Final Takeaways

- The bureaus do not approve or deny; they supply the data that drives decisions
- Your Middle Credit Score is only as strong as the **least accurate bureau**
- Reports differ for normal reasons (coverage and timing), but errors must be corrected fast
- Monitoring is not an obsession; it is protection and a timing advantage
- Disputes work when they are specific, documented, and followed through
- Locks and alerts do not raise scores, but they prevent damage that costs months to undo
- Alternative data is expanding, but fundamentals and accuracy still run the system

Maximizing Financial Opportunities Through Credit

Using Credit to Expand Access, Options, and Timing

Your Middle Credit Score® is more than just a number; it is a key that unlocks access. Access to better rates. Access to better terms. Access to approvals that can shape the next five, ten, or twenty years of your life. In real-world lending, your Middle Credit Score often determines whether you are negotiating from strength or simply hoping to be accepted. It influences the interest you pay, the fees you are charged, the programs available to you, and how much flexibility you have when life presents an opportunity.

WHAT IS YOUR MIDDLE CREDIT SCORE?

I have watched people miss out on homes they could afford, not because they did not have income, but because their credit file had one weak link that could have been fixed in advance. I have also seen clients walk into underwriting with confidence because they understood what lenders were looking for and they prepared early. That is the difference this chapter is designed to create. Not perfection. Preparation. Not guesswork. Strategy.

Improving and maintaining a strong Middle Credit Score® does not happen by chance; it happens by decisions repeated consistently. The things that build credit are not complicated. Still, it does require discipline: pay on time, keep utilization under control, avoid unnecessary inquiries, and know when to open credit and when to sit still. Most importantly, learn to see your report through a lender's eyes - not just through a consumer app. When you understand this, credit becomes less emotional and more tactical.

What most people do not realize is that credit is not only about borrowing money. Credit is about pricing. It is about leverage. It is about how expensive it is to be you in the financial system. A stronger Middle Credit Score® can reduce your borrowing costs, lower your insurance premiums, simplify rental approvals, and open access to products that reward you for spending you are already doing. That is why I call it financial efficiency. It does not just help you get approved; it enables you to keep more of your money.

This chapter is built to help you use your Middle Credit Score® as a tool, not a mystery. If your goal is homeownership, we're going to talk about how credit affects rate and qualification, and what to do months before you apply, not weeks. If your goal is entrepreneurship, we are going to talk about how personal credit is often the first underwrite, and how to build business credit without sacrificing your personal profile. If your goal is everyday financial freedom, we are going to talk about the hidden ways credit costs you money and how strong credit quietly gives it back.

Most importantly, you will learn how to move intentionally. Credit rewards stability. It rewards consistency. It rewards the person who pays attention before applying. If you are willing to treat your Middle Credit Score® like an asset, something you protect and build, then it becomes one of the most powerful financial tools you will ever own.

Section 1: The Power of a Strong Middle Credit Score®

Your Middle Credit Score® is the score that often matters most when a lender is making a serious decision, especially in mortgage lending. It is not about the highest score you have, and it is not about the lowest score you fear. It is the middle, the median, the one that represents balance across all three bureaus. That is why it becomes such a reliable indicator in lending. It's harder to "game," and it is less likely to be distorted by a single bureau's unusual reporting.

When your Middle Credit Score is strong, lenders view you differently. You are not just an applicant; you are an asset. You are the borrower who is more likely to pay on time, less likely to default, and less likely to create risk for the bank. And in lending, risk has a price. The lower the risk you represent, the less you pay for money.

A strong Middle Credit Score often means lower interest rates, reduced fees, better program options, and faster approvals. It can reduce or eliminate specific requirements, such as higher reserve expectations or larger down payments. It can also create real leverage when comparing lenders, shopping rates, or asking for better terms. Credit is one of the few places in personal finance where improving one number can create a ripple effect across multiple areas of your life.

I have seen borrowers save tens of thousands simply by moving their Middle Credit Score into a better pricing tier before a mortgage application. That is not theory. That is math. When your interest rate drops, the savings do not appear once; they compound every month, for years, and sometimes decades. The difference between "good credit" and "great credit" is not just bragging rights. It is thousands of dollars that stay in your household instead of going to a lender.

This is not limited to mortgages; auto loans, personal loans, business lines of credit, and even certain insurance premiums can be influenced by credit-based risk scoring. A strong Middle Credit Score improves your overall financial positioning because it reduces friction. It makes approvals smoother. It keeps deposits lower. It opens premium products. It gives you options when you need options.

From My Client Files - Example 38 (Chapter 6)
Better Pricing with a strong Middle Credit Score®

Paul came to me excited and prepared to buy his first home. He had done a lot right: steady income, clean payment history, and a Middle Credit Score® of 720. On the surface, that number looked good. But what mattered was not just that he would be approved, it was how much that approval would cost him over time. That's where most borrowers miss the real conversation.

*When we compared Paul's loan pricing to someone with a 660 Middle Credit Score, the difference was not subtle; it was massive. Interest rate tiers shifted. Mortgage insurance costs changed. Over the whole life of the loan, the lower-score borrower would have paid nearly **$50,000 more** for the same house. Same purchase price. Same income. Same neighborhood. The only difference was how lenders priced perceived risk.*

That $50,000 was not theoretical. It translated into flexible money that could go toward home improvements, emergency reserves, investing, or simply peace of mind. This is what a strong Middle Credit Score® does. It does not just get you approved. It lowers the cost of your future and gives you options. When you understand this, credit stops being about "good enough" and starts being about positioning yourself to win.

Section 2: Using Your Middle Credit Score to Achieve Homeownership

Homeownership is one of the most powerful wealth-building tools available to everyday families. Its stability, its pride, its control over your living environment, and, over time, its equity. When you buy a home, however, you are not only purchasing the property. You are buying the financing terms that come with it. Your Middle Credit Score influences those terms more than most people realize.

In mortgage lending, your Middle Credit Score can impact your interest rate, your mortgage insurance costs, and sometimes your program eligibility. It can also influence how aggressively you can negotiate when comparing lenders. When your credit is strong, lenders compete for you. When your credit is weak, you compete for lenders. That shift matters.

There is also timing. Credit is not something you "fix" in the same month you apply for a mortgage, at least not if you want the best possible terms. The people who win in home financing are the ones who prepare early. They pull reports ahead of time. They pay down utilization. They avoid new inquiries. They correct errors. They create a clean, stable profile that underwriters can trust.

A common misunderstanding is thinking that "qualifying" is the goal. Qualifying is the minimum. The real goal is to qualify with strength. Strength gives you better pricing, better options, and less stress. It is the difference between barely fitting into a program and being in the driver's seat when you are choosing terms.

From My Client Files - Example 39 (Chapter 6): Simple Plan, Saved Thousands

---

I worked with a couple, Adam and Emily, whose Middle Credit Scores were around 640. They could qualify for Fair Housing Administration (FHA), but they did not want to accept higher costs if they could improve their profile. We built a six-month plan: pay down cards, remove a small error, stop unnecessary *credit activity, and stabilize. When they applied, their scores were 720. They saved nearly $15,000 in interest over the life of their loan, and they walked into closing feeling as if they had earned it, not as if they'd gotten lucky.*

That is the difference between letting credit happen to you and using it intentionally. Homeownership becomes easier when your Middle Credit Score is prepared for the moment you are ready. When it is prepared, you can shop confidently, negotiate intelligently, and choose the mortgage that supports your life instead of restricting it.

Section 3: Leveraging Credit for Business Ventures

If you are an entrepreneur, your Middle Credit Score isn't just personal, it is foundational. In the early stages of business, lenders often underwrite the person before they underwrite the company. That means your individual credit profile can determine whether your business idea gets oxygen or gets delayed.

I have worked with business owners who were brilliant, hardworking, and profitable, yet struggled to access capital because their personal credit history did not reflect stability. On paper, the lender did not see the vision. They saw risk, and risk is expensive. That is why credit becomes a form of credibility in entrepreneurship.

A strong Middle Credit Score can help you qualify for business loans, business credit cards, and lines of credit that support cash flow. It can also influence vendor relationships, equipment financing, and even leasing a commercial space. Many business owners do not realize how often personal credit factors into business decisions, especially during the first years, before the business has established its own credit history.

The smart strategy is to use personal credit to open the first doors, then transition to building business credit as quickly as possible. That means separating finances, establishing accounts in the business name, and using business credit responsibly so the company develops its own financial identity. The goal is to grow without putting your personal credit at constant risk.

From My Client Files - Example 40 (Chapter 6): Established Strong Business Credit

One of my clients, Anthony, wanted to open a specialty bakery. His Middle Credit Score was 750, which gave him leverage. He qualified for a $50,000 loan with solid terms, but the bank required personal strength to approve it. We built a plan to protect his personal score while he established business credit. Within two years, his business credit profile was strong enough to access larger financing without leaning so heavily on his personal credit. That is how credit becomes a bridge, something you use to cross into business growth, not something you carry forever as a burden.

If you treat your Middle Credit Score like a business asset, it becomes one. It gives you options, lowers your costs, and increases your ability to move when opportunity arises, and in business, timing matters. The entrepreneur who can move quickly often wins.

Section 4: Enhancing Everyday Financial Freedom

Most people only think about credit when they are trying to buy something big. But credit shows up in small places, quiet places where it can either cost you money or save you money. That is why your Middle Credit Score is not just a borrowing tool. It is an everyday financial advantage.

A strong credit profile can lower insurance premiums, reduce or eliminate utility deposits, simplify rental approvals, and open access to better credit cards with rewards. Those benefits do not feel dramatic at first, but over time they stack. Thirty dollars saved per month on insurance. Two hundred dollars not tied up in deposits. A lower security deposit on a rental. Cashback on expenses you already have. These are not just perks; they are cash flow improvements.

I've seen clients struggle with everyday friction because of credit. Getting denied for rentals, paying higher deposits and premiums, and feeling like everything costs more.

In many cases, it does. When your credit is weak, the financial system charges you more for being you. When your credit is strong, that extra cost drops, and life becomes smoother.

From My Client Files - Example 41 (Chapter 6): Reduced Credit Utilization

---

One client, Sue, came to me frustrated. She had been rejected for rentals; her car insurance was high, and she was tired of constantly paying extra. We built a six-month plan: reduce utilization, dispute an outdated collection, automate *payments, and stabilize. Her middle credit score increased from 610 to 730. The difference was immediate. She got approved for the rental she wanted with a reduced deposit, her insurance premium dropped by $40 a month, and she qualified for a rewards card that gave her cashback on groceries and gas.*

That is financial freedom in real form. Not luxury. Relief. Flexibility. Confidence. It starts with understanding that credit is not just for loans; it is part of your daily financial environment.

Section 5: Using Credit Strategically for Debt Management

Debt can feel heavy because it puts pressure on you. Pressure on your paycheck. Pressure on your choices. Pressure on your future. But debt can also be managed strategically when you understand how credit works and when you use the right tools without creating new damage.

Your Middle Credit Score plays a significant role in debt strategy because it influences the tools available to you and the cost of those tools. If your credit is strong, you can consolidate at lower rates. You can use balance transfers. You can negotiate interest reductions. You can refinance. If your credit is weak, you often get stuck paying more interest, which slows progress and increases frustration.

The key is to reduce interest first, then reduce principal aggressively. Interest is what keeps people trapped. When you lower the interest burden, the same monthly payment suddenly starts making real progress. That is why balance transfers and consolidation loans can be powerful if you use them with discipline, not as a reset button to keep spending.

From My Client Files - Example 42 (Chapter 6): Reduced High Credit Card Interest Rates

---

I worked with a client, Jay, who had over $20,000 in credit card debt across multiple cards. He was paying more than the minimum, but the interest rates were eating into his progress. We built a plan: move the most expensive balances to a 0% card, consolidate what remained at a lower fixed rate, then use the avalanche method to attack the highest interest first. Within 18 months, the debt was gone, his Middle Credit Score improved by over 50 points, and he positioned himself for a stronger home loan later.

That is what strategic credit use looks like. It is not just getting out of debt; it is getting out while improving your profile, so the next chapter of your financial life becomes easier, not harder.

Section 6: Building Wealth Through Credit

Credit is often misunderstood as something you use to buy things. In reality, credit can be used to build things when it's used responsibly, intentionally, and with a long-term plan. A strong Middle Credit Score can reduce borrowing costs, and when borrowing costs are lower, more money remains available for growth. That's one of the foundations of wealth-building.

Wealth is not only about income. It is about how efficiently you can turn income into assets. Credit helps with that when it allows you to acquire appreciating assets under favorable terms. Real estate is the clearest example. A strong Middle Credit Score can put you in a position to buy a property at a lower rate, which improves cash flow, accelerates equity growth, and increases long-term returns.

Credit also plays a role in accessing home equity tools like HELOCs or cash-out refinancing when used with discipline and purpose. These tools can fund renovations that increase property value, down payments on additional properties, or even business investments. Used wisely, they become leverage. Used recklessly, they become a risk. The difference is always the plan.

From My Client Files - Example 43 (Chapter 6): Invested in Rental Properties

One client, Evelyn, had a 750 Middle Credit Score and wanted to build wealth through rental properties. We created a strategy: secure a favorable loan on a duplex, build equity, leverage that equity responsibly to renovate and increase income, then reinvest profits into the next property. Within a few years, she owned multiple rental properties generating consistent cash flow. That was not luck. That was credit used as a wealth tool paired with discipline and long-term thinking.

When you see credit through that lens, it changes how you treat it. You stop thinking, "What can I buy?" and start thinking, "What can I build?" That shift marks the beginning of financial independence.

Section 7: Avoiding Pitfalls While Leveraging Credit

Credit can absolutely elevate your life, but credit can also punish shortcuts. I have seen it happen to good people with good intentions. They were not reckless. They were simply uninformed, moving too fast, or making decisions emotionally rather than strategically. The problem is that credit does not judge intentions. It judges behavior. It measures risk based on patterns, and when you slip into specific patterns, high utilization, missed payments, too many new accounts, too much debt too fast, the system responds immediately.

One of the most common pitfalls is overconfidence. A person gets approved for a credit line, then assumes approval equals affordability. It does not. Approval means the lender is willing to take the risk, often because they believe they will be paid back with interest. But the borrower's real job is to make sure the debt fits inside their life without strain. When credit becomes a monthly stressor, it stops being a tool and starts becoming a trap.

Another pitfall is confusing "access" with "strategy." Just because you can take out a loan, run up a card, or use equity does not mean you should. Strategy requires a purpose, a plan, and an exit. Especially when it comes to wealth-building, entrepreneurship, or using leverage, credit should never be used without knowing how you will pay it down, how long you will carry it, and what the total cost will be if life does not go perfectly.

Then there are the silent pitfalls of fees, terms, and fine print. Many people focus on the payment and ignore the structure. Variable rates can rise. Promotional periods end. Balance transfer fees quietly add cost. Deferred interest can hit like a surprise bill. If you do not understand those mechanics, you can end up paying far more than you expected, even when you "did everything right."

The biggest truth I have learned over decades is simple: credit rewards calm. It rewards stability. It rewards the person who moves intentionally and does not panic. When you borrow with discipline, keep balances controlled, understand your terms, and align credit decisions with your long-term goals, credit becomes one of the most powerful tools you can use to build freedom.

7 Actionable Steps to Avoid Common Credit Pitfalls

1. **Avoid Overborrowing**
    Only take on debt that comfortably fits your budget, not just your approval limit. Before you borrow, calculate the payment, the worst-case scenario, and whether you can still breathe financially if something changes.

2. **Keep Utilization Under Control**
    Even if you pay on time, high balances can drag your Middle Credit Score down fast. As a rule, keep revolving utilization under 30%, and if you're preparing for a significant loan, aim to push it even lower.

3. **Watch for Fees and Hidden Costs**
    Balance transfer fees, annual fees, closing costs, prepayment penalties, and late fees can turn "good" credit use into expensive credit use. Read the terms carefully and ask questions until you fully understand the cost.

4. **Understand Your Loan Terms Before You Sign**
    Know whether your rate is fixed or variable, how interest is calculated, what happens if you miss a payment, and whether there are penalties or changes after the promotional period ends.

5. **Stay Disciplined with Credit Spending**
    Do not use credit to fund a lifestyle your income cannot

support. If you use cards for rewards, pay them off monthly, because credit should enhance your life not, inflate it.

6. **Limit New Credit Activity Before Major Financing**
   If you're planning a mortgage, auto loan, or business funding, avoid opening new accounts and avoid unnecessary inquiries in the months leading up to your application.

7. **Keep Your Long-Term Goals in View**
   Ask yourself one question before taking on debt: *Does this move me closer to where I want to be, or does it create pressure that delays my future?* If it delays your future, it's not a strategy.

Section 8: Real World Wins – How Strategy Beats Hope

From My Client Files - Example 44 (Chapter 6):
Hope Without a Plan (And Why Strategy Always Wins)

A former client, Chris, came to me after maxing out multiple cards to fund a business idea. He was not careless, he was hopeful. Now, I want you to hear what I'm about to say with no judgment, because a lot of good people get caught right here: **hope does not protect your file. A plan does.** *What happened next was predictable, not because Chris was "bad with money," but because the system responds to math, not emotion.*

Utilization spiked. Minimum payments got heavier. Stress rose. As a result, his Middle Credit Score slid under 600 not overnight, but fast enough that by the time he realized what was happening, the damage was already pricing him out of better options. That drop did not just hurt his confidence. It removed flexibility at the exact moment he needed it.

We consolidated the debt, built a real budget, and rebuilt stability one month at a time. Within a year, his Middle Credit Score climbed back into the high 600s, and the most significant change was not just the score. It was his mindset. He stopped using credit like a lifeline and started using it like a tool. The lesson was not "never use credit."
The lesson was **never to use credit without a plan.**

From My Client Files - Example 45 (Chapter 6): Buying a First Home

---

Wendy wanted to buy her first home but felt stuck at a Middle Credit Score of 650. We reviewed her file and found the usual culprits: high utilization, a negative item that should have been corrected, and inconsistent payment timing. Over six months, she paid down her cards below 30%, set up automated payments, and disputed an outdated collection. When she applied for a mortgage, her Middle Credit Score was 720. That bump did not just get her approved, it got her priced better. Her rate dropped by about a whole point compared to what she would have paid, saving her roughly $40,000 over the life of the loan. She did not change her income; she changed her positioning.

From My Client Files - Example 46 (Chapter 6): The Client Who Won by Doing Less

---

Some of the best credit outcomes I've ever seen did not come from aggressive action; they came from restraint. Mark did not open new cards to "boost available credit." He did not finance furniture, upgrade a car, or chase quick fixes. Instead, he deliberately decided to stop making random moves. For 60–90 days before their application, they treated their credit profile like a protected asset, not a playground.

Mark kept balances consistently low, paid every account on time, and avoided unnecessary inquiries. Nothing flashy. Nothing emotional. Just disciplined behavior repeated quietly, and that discipline mattered. When underwriting reviewed the file, there were no red flags, no volatility, and no questions that slowed the process down. The profile told a simple story: stability, predictability, low risk.

This is the lesson most consumers miss. You do not win credit decisions by doing more; you win by doing the right things at the right time. Boring credit is powerful credit because it gives lenders confidence, and confidence drives better pricing, smoother approvals, and fewer surprises. The goal is not activity. The goal is control.

From My Client Files - Example 47 (Chapter 6): Accumulated High Credit Card Debt

---

Rachel was not reckless; she was overwhelmed by momentum working against her. Over time, high-interest credit card balances piled up to nearly $10,000, and even though she was making payments, most of her money was being eaten up by interest. The balances were not dropping fast enough to create relief, and emotionally, she felt stuck. This is where many people give up or start making desperate moves. Instead, Rachel paused and chose strategy over panic.

We evaluated her options and identified a 0% APR balance transfer with an 18-month promotional window. Yes, there was a transfer fee, but the math mattered more than the emotion. The interest savings far outweighed the upfront cost. The key rule was discipline: this was not a debt reshuffling; it was a payoff plan with a deadline. Rachel treated the promotional period like a countdown clock, paying aggressively and consistently until the balance hit zero before interest ever returned.

As the balances dropped, two things happened simultaneously. Her utilization improved, which lifted her Middle Credit Score by roughly 40 points, and the mental weight she had been carrying disappeared. That is what strategic credit use looks like. Credit was not a crutch; it was a tool used intentionally once and then put away. When credit is used with a plan and an exit strategy, it creates momentum instead of stress.

From My Client Files - Example 48 (Chapter 6): HELOC Loan Buys Investment Property

Karen had built substantial equity in her primary residence and wanted to invest in a rental property without liquidating other assets. With a Middle Credit Score near 770, she qualified for a HELOC at a favorable rate. Instead of viewing the line of credit as discretionary money, she treated it as structured leverage. She used the HELOC to purchase and renovate a small duplex, keeping tight control over draw timing, renovation costs, and repayment structure.

The rental income from the duplex covered the HELOC payment, allowing the debt to service itself while the property appreciated. As the renovation increased the property's value, Karen effectively converted home equity into an income-producing asset. Her net worth grew not because she took on risk mindlessly, but because the cost of capital was low enough to make the numbers work.

What made this strategy viable was not just equity; it was credit quality. A weaker Middle Credit Score would have resulted in higher rates, tighter terms, or denial altogether, turning the same plan into an expensive or unworkable gamble. Karen's strong middle score did not create the opportunity by itself, but it made disciplined leverage affordable. And when leverage is inexpensive, it becomes a tool for growth rather than a source of financial stress.

From My Client Files - Example 49 (Chapter 6):
When Consolidation Becomes a Weapon (Not a Trap)

---

*Another client was drowning in revolving minimums not because they were reckless, but because the interest was eating them alive. We consolidated the debt, created a real spending plan, and protected the habits that rebuild credit: payment history first, utilization second, and zero unnecessary inquiries. Within a year, their Middle Credit Score recovered into the high 600s, and they finally had options again. The lesson was not "debt is evil." The lesson was: **if you consolidate without discipline, you're delaying pain. If you consolidate with discipline, you're buying freedom.***

Bottom line: A strong Middle Credit Score creates options, and when you have options, you choose the best path instead of the only path.

From My Client Files – Example 50 (Chapter 6):
Restored Access to Better Financing

Marcus, a former client, came to me after leaning on several cards to launch a side venture. He was not reckless, he was optimistic however, optimism does not reduce borrowing costs. Utilization surged, the payments tightened, and his Middle Credit Score fell below 590. That drop did not only sting emotionally; it removed access to affordable financing when he needed it most. We reorganized the balances, built a realistic budget, and restored stability. Within a year, his Middle Credit Score rose back into the high 680s, and he finally had choices again when pressure replaced patience and discipline. The lesson was not "avoid credit." The lesson was "never use credit without a plan."

These examples all point to the same truth: a strong Middle Credit Score creates options, and when you have options, you can choose the best path instead of the only path.

Chapter 6 Closing: Credit Is Leverage When You Use It on Purpose

If there's one mindset shift I want you to take from this chapter, it's this: credit is not a label, it is leverage. It is the difference between walking into a major decision hoping someone says yes, versus walking in with options and negotiating power. Your Middle Credit Score does not just influence whether you are approved; it influences how expensive the approval becomes. And over the course of a mortgage, a business loan, or even years of everyday financial life, that cost difference adds up to real money that either stays in your household or leaks out through interest, fees, and higher pricing.

I have watched consumers change outcomes without changing income. They did not get a raise; they got strategic. They lowered utilization, protected payment history, corrected errors, and stayed calm in the months that mattered. That is what strong credit really is: peaceful, consistent behavior that makes lenders trust your file. When your profile is stable, you stop paying the "high-cost tax" for borrowing money, and you start using credit as a tool to reduce debt, build wealth, fund opportunity, and move through life with less friction.

In the next chapter, we are going to make this even more practical, on how to prepare your credit before major financing decisions, so you are never trying to fix your profile while an underwriter is watching.

The One Action Framework

The "Opportunity Readiness" Plan (30 / 60 / 90 Days)

Days 1–30: Stabilize Your Position (Stop the Leaks)

Pull all three bureau reports and identify your Middle Credit Score today. Make a list of the top three factors holding it back (utilization, late payments, errors, collections, too many inquiries, thin file). Set autopay on every account (minimums at least) and stop new credit applications. If there is an obvious reporting error, dispute it with clean documentation immediately.

Days 31–60: Strengthen the Profile (Build Pricing Power)

Reduce utilization strategically, focus on the highest-utilization cards first, and push balances down below 30% (lower if you're preparing for a significant loan). Keep accounts current and protect payment history like an asset. If you're consolidating debt, do it with a plan: reduce interest first, then attack principal with discipline. Keep your credit activity quiet; no new accounts unless there's an apparent, strategic reason.

Days 61–90: Lock in Leverage (Prepare for the Snapshot)

This is the window where outcomes change. Keep your profile boring: low balances, no new inquiries, no co-signing, no last-minute spending spikes. Confirm that your reports are aligned across all three bureaus and that your Middle Credit Score accurately reflects your actual behavior. If a primary application is coming, treat these 90 days like a launch period. Calm credit creates confident approvals and better terms.

Chapter 6 Final Takeaways

- Your Middle Credit Score is leveraged; it affects approvals, rates, fees, and options
- Strong credit lowers the cost of money and keeps more cash in your household.
- Homeownership is won months before application through stability, low utilization, and clean reports
- Entrepreneurs are often personally underwritten. First personal credit opens early business doors
- Strong credit reduces everyday friction through deposits, approvals, and pricing advantages
- Debt tools can work (consolidation, balance transfers) only when paired with discipline and a plan
- Wealth-building becomes more efficient when credit reduces borrowing costs and supports controlled leverage
- The biggest pitfalls come from emotional borrowing, high utilization, and ignoring terms and fees
- Approval is not affordability. Your budget decides what's safe, not the lender's limit
- Credit rewards calm: consistency and predictability produce long-term financial power

Maintaining Financial Stability Through Credit Awareness

Taking Control Through Consistent Credit Awareness

Financial stability is not just about having money in the bank; it's about being able to breathe. It is about knowing that if life happens, you will not collapse under it. Over the years, I have watched people with high incomes struggle because they had no system, no plan, and no awareness of how their credit and money choices were shaping their future. By contrast, I have also watched people with modest incomes build strong, stable lives because they understood one truth: stability is built, not wished for.

Credit awareness is the difference between reacting and leading. When you understand your credit profile, you stop being surprised by denials, higher rates, deposits, and "computer says no" moments. Your credit becomes a dashboard, not a mystery. You begin to see your financial behavior the way lenders see it: as patterns. Those patterns tell a story. And once you understand how that story is written, you gain the power to rewrite it on purpose.

One of the most overlooked parts of stability is that credit touches everyday life. It can influence where you live, what you pay for insurance, how much a lender charges you for the same loan, and even whether a landlord or employer sees you as dependable. This is why credit awareness is bigger than "what is my score?" It is about understanding what's behind the score, what is helping it, what is hurting it, and what needs attention before you make a significant move.

In this chapter, we are going to connect credit awareness to something most people skip: goals. Not vague goals, tangible goals. Goals that have timelines, milestones, and measurable progress. When your goals are clear, your behavior becomes clearer. Your spending becomes more intentional. Your credit habits become more disciplined, and stability becomes less about luck and more about leadership, your leadership.

Section 1: Setting Clear Financial Goals

Financial stability begins long before you see the result. It starts when you decide what matters most and stop allowing your financial life to be driven by emergencies, impulses, or short-term comfort. In my experience, the people who achieve lasting stability don't necessarily have the most money; they have the most clarity. They know what they are building, and they make decisions that support that build.

Goals are powerful because they turn credit into a tool instead of a temptation. Without goals, credit becomes reactive: you borrow because you're short, you swipe because you are stressed, you apply because you are hoping. With goals, credit becomes strategic: you use it to reduce costs, to access opportunities, and to protect your future. That's the shift that changes everything.

The truth is, your Middle Credit Score® does not improve because you want it to. It improves because your behaviors align with a plan, and a plan only works when it is connected to something you care about: homeownership, debt freedom, business growth, family security, retirement, and generational wealth.

Clear goals also protect you from distraction. Financial life will always throw noise at you: sales, offers, lifestyle pressure, unexpected bills, and emotional spending triggers. Goals filter that noise. They help you say "no" today, so you can say "yes" to what matters tomorrow.

Short-term goals build momentum. Mid-term goals build structure. Long-term goals build a legacy. When those three levels are aligned, stability becomes a natural outcome of your routine.

From My Client Files - Example 51 (Chapter 7): From Living without a Financial Plan, to Living with a Financial Plan

---

Jason and Linda did not come to me in crisis because they were careless; they came in overwhelmed because everything felt reactive. Credit card balances were climbing, savings were thin, and every unexpected expense felt like a setback. They were not failing financially; they were operating without a roadmap, and without a plan, even good intentions turn into stress.

The first step was not aggressive debt payoff or score chasing. It was clarity. We defined what they wanted: homeownership, family stability, and fewer financial surprises. From there, we built three layers of goals: short-term stability, mid-term credit strength, and long-term security. They started with the basics: a realistic budget they could follow, a starter emergency fund to absorb shocks, and a debt strategy that reduced pressure instead of creating it.

As the plan took hold, everything else followed. Small wins created momentum. Momentum created consistency. And consistency naturally improved their Middle Credit Scores. Within two years, Jason and Linda weren't hoping things would work out; they were living inside a system that supported them. That is the difference a real financial plan makes: it turns uncertainty into structure, and structure into confidence.

Section 2: Building a Strong Financial Foundation

Goals without a foundation will always feel fragile. You can have the best dream in the world, but if your financial foundation is unstable, that dream becomes stressful rather than empowering. A strong foundation is what allows you to move forward without fear. It gives you options. It gives you resilience. It gives you the ability to handle life without letting life wreck your credit.

In my career, I have seen the same pattern repeatedly: when people stabilize the basics, their credit improves as a byproduct. They do not have to obsess over the score because the behaviors that create stability are the same behaviors that create credit strength: on-time payments, controlled utilization, fewer emergencies, and fewer desperate credit decisions.

A foundation also removes the panic from borrowing. When you have savings and a plan, you do not use credit out of fear. You use it out of strategy. That difference between fear vs. strategy is where many people either build stability or lose it.

A solid foundation includes budgeting, emergency savings, debt control, and routine credit monitoring. It also provides self-awareness: tracking your habits, learning your triggers, and building accountability.

From My Client Files - Example 52 (Chapter 7): Built a Stronger Foundation

---

Kira did not come to me recklessly; she came exhausted. High-interest credit card balances were eating her cash flow, there was no emergency fund to fall back on, and her credit reports had been ignored for years, not out of denial, but out of burnout. She felt like she was constantly reacting, putting out one financial fire after another, with no space to get ahead. The problem was not intelligence or effort. It was the absence of a foundation.

We did not start with drastic cuts or unrealistic rules. We began with a structure she could live with. A budget that did not feel like punishment. A small, achievable emergency fund goal, so the next unexpected expense wouldn't go straight onto a credit card. A debt strategy that focused on early wins, not perfection, to build momentum. As pressure decreased, clarity increased. And as clarity improved, consistency followed.

Within a year, Kira's financial life looked completely different. She had savings. Credit emergencies stopped dictating her decisions. Utilization dropped. Her Middle Credit Score strengthened not because she chased it, but because the behavior underneath it finally stabilized. That is the power of a factual foundation: when it holds, everything built on top of it gets stronger without constant effort.

Section 3: Staying Informed and Educated

Financial stability requires awareness, and awareness requires education. The financial world changes, interest rates shift, scoring models evolve, lender requirements tighten or loosen, and consumer protections get updated. If you are not staying informed, you can do "the same things" and get different outcomes simply because the rules around you have changed.

Staying informed does not mean becoming a financial expert overnight. It means developing a habit of learning enough to make confident decisions. It means understanding what impacts your Middle Credit Score, what lenders look for, what behaviors move your score, and what behaviors quietly damage it.

Education is also protection. When you understand credit and lending, you are less likely to be manipulated by marketing, pressured into bad terms, or surprised by fees. You become the person who asks the right questions before signing anything.

Credit awareness also includes knowing what is on your reports and why. Too many people assume "no news is good news" until they apply for something essential and discover an error, an outdated item, or a suspicious account. Stability is built by catching problems early, not finding them late.

From My Client Files - Example 53 (Chapter 7): Untimely Job Loss

---

Angela lost her job unexpectedly and felt like everything was slipping at once. Her first fear was not just income; it was what the interruption might do to her credit and future options. She had some savings, but she did not fully understand how credit behavior during a disruption could either protect her or quietly create new problems. Like many people in transition, she assumed that once income stopped, damage was inevitable.

Instead of reacting emotionally, we built a simple, repeatable routine. She monitored her Middle Credit Score®, reviewed all three bureau reports for accuracy, and learned how to prioritize minimum payments, utilization control, and timing. We also focused on education, understanding what mattered most during uncertainty and what could safely wait. That structure gave her clarity when everything else felt uncertain.

What changed was not just her credit profile; it was her decision-making. Because her credit remained stable, Angela avoided panic-driven choices like closing accounts, overusing credit, or skipping payments to "buy time." When she returned to work, her profile was intact, her options were open, and her confidence was earned. The lesson here is critical: credit awareness does not just help you advance; it protects you when life disrupts your plans. Stability during stress is not accidental; it's built through knowledge and routine.

Section 4: Harnessing the Power of Your Middle Credit Score®

Your Middle Credit Score is one of the most practical financial tools you have. It can reduce borrowing costs, expand your options, and position you as a lower-risk borrower. But the power of the score is not in the number itself; it's in how you use it.

A strong Middle Credit Score creates leverage. It allows you to negotiate. It will enable you to choose. It allows you to access programs, terms, and opportunities that other borrowers pay more for. What most people don't realize is that the "extra" they pay because of weak credit is not just interest; it is insurance premiums, deposits, fees, and limited choices.

Harnessing your Middle Credit Score starts with treating it like a living profile. It needs monitoring, maintenance, and occasional correction. It requires intentional habits. It needs protection from unnecessary inquiries, high balances, and missed payments.

When you understand your score, you stop guessing. You stop hoping. You start planning. And planning is what creates stability.

From My Client Files - Example 54 (Chapter 7):
Maintain Middle Credit Score® Awareness

Anna avoided her credit for years because it intimidated her. She assumed that if something were wrong, it would feel overwhelming to fix, so she chose distance instead of understanding. That avoidance did not stop her from achieving her goals; it just delayed them. When she began exploring options to fund a small business, she quickly learned that her Middle Credit Score® would be one of the first filters lenders used to decide whether to move the conversation forward.

Once Anna understood how the Middle Credit Score worked and why lenders relied on it, everything changed. She stopped treating credit like a judgment and started treating it like a system. She began tracking her score monthly, reviewed all three bureau reports for accuracy, corrected reporting errors, and adjusted her habits with intention. Her focus wasn't perfection; it was consistency. Each minor correction reduced uncertainty and gave her more precise control over outcomes.

Within six months, her Middle Credit Score rose by more than 50 points. But the fundamental shift was not just numerical, it was psychological. Credit no longer felt intimidating; it felt manageable. The loan that once felt out of reach became realistic, not because of a shortcut, but because awareness replaced avoidance. Anna's experience reinforces a core truth of financial stability: when you understand the system, you stop fearing it, and when fear disappears, progress becomes sustainable.

Section 5: Building Generational Wealth

Financial stability becomes truly powerful when it extends beyond you. Generational wealth is not only about money, but it is also about options and education being passed down. It is about making sure your children do not have to start from scratch. It is about reducing the financial pain cycles that repeat in families when nobody is taught how credit works.

A strong Middle Credit Score helps lower the cost of building assets. It can help you buy income-generating real estate, secure favorable financing, and free up cash flow to invest, rather than waste on interest. Over time, those savings compound into real wealth.

Generational wealth also requires structure: estate planning, tax-advantaged accounts, disciplined investing, and teaching financial literacy early. When younger generations grow up understanding budgets, credit, and investing, they do not just inherit assets, they inherit competence.

From My Client Files - Example 55 (Chapter 7): Teaching Your Kids by Example

James did not just want better credit; he wanted a different outcome for his family. Early in his career, he realized that the conversations he wished he'd had growing up were not about money itself, but about how decisions compound over time. With a strong Middle Credit Score®, he qualified for favorable financing on rental properties, built steady income streams, and created financial breathing room that most families never experience. But the real impact showed up at home.

Instead of shielding his kids from money conversations, James included them. He explained budgeting in real terms. He talked openly about why keeping utilization low mattered, why payments were automated, and why credit was not something to fear or abuse. They watched him plan purchases rather than react to them. They saw patience rewarded with better terms. Credit became normal, not mysterious.

By the time college approached, the family had options rooted in years of disciplined credit management and intentional planning. Tuition decisions weren't driven by panic or desperation over debt. They were strategic. What James passed down was not just assets or income; it was financial literacy lived out loud. His kids did not just hear advice; they saw it modeled. And that's how generational change begins, not with lectures, but with consistent example.

Section 6: Staying Motivated on Your Financial Path

Financial stability is not achieved in one heroic moment. It is achieved through repeated, sometimes boring consistency, and that is why motivation matters. Motivation is what keeps you going when progress feels slow. It is what keeps you disciplined when life tempts you to quit.

The most successful clients I have ever worked with learned how to celebrate progress. They stopped waiting for the "big win". They started recognizing the smaller wins, such as paying down a card, building the first $1,000 in savings, moving utilization under 30%, correcting a report error, and raising their Middle Credit Score by 10 points. Those smaller wins build identity. They make you the kind of person who follows through.

Motivation also grows when you can see your progress. That is why tracking matters. Whether you use a journal, an app, or a simple monthly check-in, visibility fuels consistency, and consistency is what builds stability.

Setbacks will happen. Motivation does not mean you never fall off track; it means you know how to get back on track quickly, without shame or panic.

From My Client Files - Example 56 (Chapter 7): One Financial Plan Produced a Stronger Future Outcome

---

Mary and Steve did not fail financially; they were tested. Unexpected medical expenses arrived at the worst possible time, and emotionally, it felt like everything they had worked for was unraveling. When they came back to the plan, the first thing we did was not adjust numbers, it was reset the perspective. We laid out the facts: debt balances were already down, their Middle Credit Scores had improved meaningfully, and their habits were far stronger than they had been before the setback. The foundation was still there.

Once they saw that progress had not been erased, motivation returned. We adjusted timelines, protected payment history, kept utilization under control, and stayed disciplined through the recovery period. They did not abandon the plan; they finished it. Because they did, they reached homeownership with confidence. The lesson is simple but powerful: strong plans do not prevent setbacks. They prevent setbacks from becoming permanent.

Section 7: Action Plan for Ongoing Credit Awareness

Financial stability is not something you achieve once and then forget about. It is a living system, one that needs consistent attention, just like your health. The goal is not to obsess over your credit, but to stay aware enough that you are never surprised. Most credit damage does not come from one dramatic mistake; it comes from drifting and missing minor warning signs, letting balances creep up, and ignoring a report until you need a loan. Stability is protected by routine.

Ongoing credit awareness works best when it is simple, repeatable, and tied to a schedule. You do not need a complex spreadsheet. You need a rhythm: review, correct, improve, protect.

Section 8: Protecting Stability Through Smart Credit Safeguards

Credit stability is not just built; it must be protected. In today's world, threats to stability can come from identity theft, data breaches, predatory offers, misleading terms, or even autopay mistakes. Smart safeguards create peace of mind by reducing the risk that avoidable problems undo your progress.

When you treat your credit like an asset, you protect it like one. You lock what needs locking. You monitor what needs monitoring. You build guardrails so you do not have to rely on willpower. Structure does the heavy lifting.

Section 9: Credit Awareness in Action

From My Client Files - Example 57 (Chapter 7):
The Monthly Credit Routine That Prevented a Mortgage Surprise

---

Derrick was not reacting to a problem; he was preparing to avoid one. He knew he wanted to buy a home within the next year, so instead of checking his credit randomly or only when something felt wrong, we set a simple rule: one scheduled "credit day" every month. Same process, same checklist review, balances, scan for new accounts, confirm payment history, and compare bureau data. It was not complicated, but it was consistent.

Three months into that routine, Derrick spotted a new account he did not recognize. Because he caught it early, the solution was clean and controlled. He froze his credit, disputed the account immediately, and documented everything. No cascade of damage. No underwriting surprise. By the time he applied for the mortgage, his profile was stable, accurate, and lender ready. That is the real power of routine: it turns what could have been a crisis into a footnote.

From My Client Files - Example 58 (Chapter 7):
Protecting Progress During a High-Spend Season

Tanya had done the hard work. Her Middle Credit Score® was improving steadily, her payment history was clean, and her utilization had finally come under control. But every year, like clockwork, the holiday season disrupted her progress. Gift spending pushed balances higher, statements closed with elevated utilization, and her score dropped, sometimes taking months to recover. The problem wasn't irresponsibility. It was timing.

Instead of telling her to "spend less" or skip the season altogether, we put a simple safeguard in place: **mid-cycle payments during high-spend**

months. *By paying balances down before statements closed, her utilization never spiked on paper, even if spending temporarily increased. The result was immediate. Her score stayed stable, her momentum continued, and she didn't have to sacrifice family traditions to protect her credit.*

What Tanya learned and what most borrowers never realize is that credit scoring does not punish spending; it punishes reported exposure. High-spend seasons are not the enemy. Unmanaged reporting cycles are. Once she understood that distinction, holidays stopped being a credit setback and became just another planned expense. Stability didn't come from avoiding life; it came from understanding how the system measures risk and adjusting behavior at the right moment.

From My Client Files - Example 59 (Chapter 7): *Autopay Helped, But Alerts Protected the Score*

Luis did what many financially responsible people are advised to do: he set up autopay and assumed the system would handle the rest. For the most part, it worked. But one month, a surprise expense lowered his checking account balance just enough for the payment to fail. Autopay didn't process, and without safeguards, that single miss could have resulted in a late fee and unnecessary damage to his Middle Credit Score®.

What saved Luis wasn't autopay, it was awareness. Real-time alerts notified him immediately that the payment hadn't gone through. He made the payment manually the same day, preventing a late mark from ever being reported. The difference wasn't luck. It was redundant. Autopay handled consistency, but alerts addressed the reality of unexpected moments when systems fail and life intervenes.

This experience reinforces an important lesson: autopay is a tool, not a guarantee. Proper credit stability comes from layered protection. When automation is paired with monitoring and alerts, you're no longer relying on a single system to behave perfectly. You're actively protecting your credit from minor disruptions that can have outsized consequences. That's how strong credit is maintained, not by assumption, but by design.

From My Client Files - Example 60 (Chapter 7): The Credit Freeze That Stopped an Identity Crisis

Monica learned that her personal information had been exposed in a large-scale data breach, and, like most people, her first reaction was fear. But instead of freezing emotionally, she froze her credit. She understood that identity protection isn't about waiting for damage to show up; it's about preventing access before it happens. Within hours, she placed credit freezes with all three bureaus, set fraud alerts, and documented every step so she could respond quickly if anything surfaced.

Because she acted early, no fraudulent accounts were ever opened in her name. More importantly, Monica learned that credit stability is not just about what you do when things go right; it is about how prepared you are when something goes wrong. That single decision protected her Middle Credit Score®, eliminated months of cleanup, and gave her peace of mind. Prevention did not just save her credit; it preserved her control.

Steps Monica Took to Protect Her Credit

1. ***Placed a credit freeze with all three bureaus*** *to prevent any new accounts from being opened without her authorization*
2. ***Updated all financial account passwords****, prioritizing email, banking, and credit-related logins*
3. ***Enabled two-factor authentication (2FA)*** *on every account that supported it*
4. ***Reviewed her credit reports*** *to confirm no unauthorized activity had already occurred*
5. ***Set up ongoing alerts*** *to monitor for attempted inquiries or account changes*

Two weeks later, someone attempted to open a new account in her name. The application was automatically blocked because of the freeze. No inquiry posted. No account was opened. No damage was done. What could have undone years of progress became a non-event, not because the threat did not exist, but because the safeguards were already in place.

This is what credit awareness looks like in real life. Monica did not wait for confirmation of harm before acting; she assumed responsibility for prevention. A credit freeze does not fix problems after they happen; it stops them from happening at all. In an era where data exposure is no longer rare, protection is no longer optional. Credit strength is not just built through good habits; it is preserved through decisive action when risk appears.

From My Client Files - Example 61 (Chapter 7): The "No Random Credit" Rule That Kept Business Funding Clean

---

Aaron did not lose funding opportunities because of bad credit; he almost lost them because of unnecessary behavior. When he decided to apply for business financing within six months, we set one non-negotiable rule: no random credit activity. No impulse cards. No "just in case" financing. No inquiries that did not directly support the plan. His credit was not fragile, but it would have become fragile if he treated availability as permission.

By staying disciplined, Aaron's profile told a clear story. Utilization stayed low. Payment history stayed clean. No new accounts introduced noise or risk signals. When lenders reviewed his file, it looked intentional, stable, and decision ready. That is what strong credit looks like at the moment it matters most: not busy, not reactive, not cluttered. Just prepared.

Chapter 7 Closing: Bringing Credit Awareness into Everyday Life

Maintaining financial stability through credit awareness is not about perfection; it is about presence. It is about knowing where you stand, understanding how your decisions ripple forward, and refusing to be passive with something that directly impacts your freedom, security, and future. Throughout this chapter, you have seen that stability is built through intention: clear goals, firm foundations, ongoing awareness, and protective guardrails that prevent life's surprises from turning into credit setbacks.

When you stay engaged with your Middle Credit Score and your overall profile, you stop waiting for someone else to tell you there is a problem. You already know. You already planned. You already positioned yourself. That awareness creates confidence, and confidence changes how you move. You pursue opportunities when they arise because your profile is ready, not because you got lucky.

Small actions done consistently will always outperform big emotional decisions made under pressure. Credit awareness becomes powerful when it becomes routine, something you maintain, not something you fear. When you treat your credit like an asset worth protecting and a tool worth mastering, you don't just build stability for today; you create it for every season ahead.

In the next chapter, we will move from strategy to proof: real success stories that show what is possible when credit awareness becomes a lifestyle. These stories are not about luck. They are about people who took control, stayed disciplined, and changed

their financial trajectory by understanding the power of their
Middle Credit Score and using it intentionally.

The One Action Framework

The "Stability System" to Build Credit Awareness as a Lifestyle Plan (30 / 60 / 90 Days)

Days 1-30: Create the Rhythm (Awareness Without Overwhelm)

1. Pick one monthly "Credit Day" and commit to it.
2. Check your Middle Credit Score and track utilization.
3. Set autopay for minimum payments on every account.
4. Turn on alerts for due dates, hefty charges, and payment confirmations.
5. Freeze your credit if you're not actively applying for new credit.

Days 31-60: Strengthen the Guardrails (Stability Through Structure)

1. Push utilization below 30% (and lower if a significant goal is coming).
2. Build a small "stability buffer" emergency fund (even if it is modest).
3. Review one bureau report carefully and note any errors or outdated items.
4. Dispute errors immediately and document everything in a simple log.

5. Create your personal "Credit Rules" list (non-negotiables you follow).

Days 61-90: Align Credit with the Life You're Building (Opportunity Ready)

1. Ask quarterly: "Is my profile positioned for what I want next?"
2. Avoid random new credit and unnecessary inquiries.
3. Keep credit boring before major moves: low balances, no new accounts, no surprises.
4. Use mid-cycle payments during high-spend months to protect utilization.
5. Measure progress and celebrate the wins because stability is built through consistency.

Credit Awareness as a Stability System: Final Awareness

Financial stability is not created by income alone; awareness, structure, and repeatable habits produce it. Credit awareness shifts you from reacting to economic problems to preventing them. When you understand your Middle Credit Score, monitor it consistently, and protect it intentionally, stability becomes a lifestyle rather than a temporary phase.

This chapter reinforces a core truth: **credit damage usually comes from neglect, not catastrophe**. The people who maintain long-term financial stability are not perfect; they are present. They check in. They correct early. They build guardrails so one surprise does not undo years of progress.

Treating your credit as an asset, something you review, protect, and align with your goals, gives you confidence, flexibility, and control. Stability doesn't require constant effort; it requires consistent attention.

Chapter 7 Final Takeaways

• Financial stability is built through systems, not willpower
• Credit awareness prevents surprises that derail long-term goals
• The Middle Credit Score should be monitored like a dashboard, not feared
• Clear goals turn credit from temptation into a strategic tool
• Strong foundations reduce panic-driven credit decisions
• Small, repeatable habits protect years of progress
• Safeguards matter as much as score improvement
• Motivation is sustained by visible progress, not perfection
• Stability comes from consistency, not intensity
• Credit awareness turns financial stress into financial leadership

Real-Life Success Stories and Lessons Learned

Inspiration Through Real-Life Examples

The path to financial empowerment is rarely linear. It is shaped by setbacks, breakthroughs, discipline, and moments of decision that force people to either surrender control or reclaim it. Over the course of my career, I have worked with individuals from every financial background imaginable, people rebuilding after bankruptcy, families navigating medical crises, professionals blindsided by identity theft, and first-time buyers who simply never understood how credit really worked. What unites their stories is not luck or privilege, but the moment they chose awareness over avoidance.

These stories are not included to impress you with outcomes; they are here to remind you that progress is possible at every starting point. Financial success is not reserved for those who "got it right early." It belongs to those who are willing to learn, adjust, and stay consistent long enough for change to take root. Everyone in this chapter faced real consequences tied to their credit profile, yet each discovered that knowledge, structure, and persistence could reverse what once felt permanent.

Credit is often spoken about in abstract terms, scores, percentages, and thresholds. Behind every number is a real person trying to build stability, protect their family, or reclaim opportunity. The stories that follow bring those numbers back to life. They show how understanding the Middle Credit Score®, correcting misinformation, and adopting disciplined habits can transform outcomes, not just financially, but also emotionally and psychologically.

As you read through these experiences, I encourage you to look beyond the details and focus on the patterns. You will see how small decisions compound, how awareness changes behavior, and how consistency eventually creates leverage. These stories are not meant to be admired from a distance; they are intended to be mirrored, adapted, and applied.

From My Client Files - Example 62 (Chapter 8): David's Method for Rebuilding After Bankruptcy.

David was a small-business owner who had poured years of effort, savings, and identity into a boutique retail shop he believed would be his long-term future. When economic conditions shifted and operating costs outpaced revenue, the pressure mounted quickly. Debt accumulated across business loans, credit cards, and a commercial lease, and eventually, bankruptcy became unavoidable. While bankruptcy provided temporary relief, it left behind a deeper challenge: a Middle Credit Score® that collapsed to 520 and a sense of being locked out of the financial system entirely.

The aftermath was more than financial. David struggled to secure housing without excessive deposits, faced higher insurance costs, and found himself unable to qualify for even modest forms of credit. Rather than withdrawing from the process, he committed to understanding it. He began educating himself about credit reporting, documenting his progress in a journal, and setting realistic milestones rather than chasing quick fixes. The focus shifted from what he had lost, to what he could rebuild.

Over time, David learned how critical accuracy, consistency, and patience were to recovery. He ensured that discharged debts were reported correctly, deliberately rebuilt his positive payment history, and diversified his credit profile responsibly. Just as important, he reframed his relationship with credit from something that once felt punitive to something he could manage strategically. Within a year, his Middle Credit Score climbed into the mid-600s, allowing him to secure financing for a new venture built on sustainability, rather than risk.

David's experience reinforces a powerful truth: bankruptcy is not a financial identity. With education, structure, and consistency, it becomes a chapter rather than a conclusion.

From My Client Files - Example 63 (Chapter 8): Tina's Fight Back After Identity Theft

Tina was diligent, organized, and financially responsible. As a healthcare worker and single mother, she understood the importance of maintaining stability. She had built a Middle Credit Score in the low 700s that supported her mortgage and long-term savings goals. That stability was shattered almost *overnight when fraudulent accounts appeared on her credit reports, sending her score plunging into the 500s without warning.*

The emotional impact was immediate. Tina felt violated, overwhelmed, and frustrated by how quickly years of responsible behavior were undermined by actions she never took. But instead of freezing in panic, she relied on her credit knowledge and took control of the process. She treated recovery as a structured project rather than a crisis, documenting every step, communication, and outcome with precision.

By staying organized and persistent, Tina corrected the inaccuracies that distorted her credit profile. More importantly, she learned how essential proactive safeguards and regular monitoring are to long-term stability. When her Middle Credit Score rebounded above its original level, she was able to refinance her mortgage and regain both financial control and peace of mind.

Tina's story highlights that credit awareness is not just about improvement, it is also about protection. Knowing how to respond quickly and methodically can mean the difference between long-term damage and complete recovery.

·From My Client Files - Example 64 (Chapter 8): Eric's Recovery After a Medical Crisis

---

Eric had always been financially responsible, balancing family obligations with steady employment and manageable credit use. That balance collapsed when a medical emergency introduced expenses his insurance did not fully cover. As bills mounted and income became strained, Eric leaned on credit cards to bridge the gap, quickly exceeding utilization thresholds and falling behind on payments. His Middle Credit Score dropped sharply, limiting his access to reliable transportation and affordable financing.

Rather than accepting the decline as permanent, Eric began reassessing both his finances and his habits. He tracked spending meticulously, distinguished needs from wants, and educated himself on how medical debt and revolving balances affected his credit profile. His journal became a record not just of numbers, but of accountability and progress.

Over time, Eric negotiated more manageable repayment structures, corrected reporting errors tied to medical billing, and simplified his obligations into a system he could control. The recovery was gradual, but measurable. As his Middle Credit Score approached the high 600s, access to affordable credit returned, and with it, confidence.

Eric's experience illustrates that even unexpected crises need not define financial futures. Awareness, structure, and persistence can transform survival into recovery, and recovery into stability.

From My Client Files – Example 65 (Chapter 8): Rebecca's Journey to Lower Insurance Costs Through Credit Awareness

Rebecca never imagined that her credit profile was quietly increasing her monthly expenses. As a homeowner and single parent, she budgeted carefully, yet each year her auto and homeowners' insurance premiums crept higher. When she finally asked her agent for an explanation, she learned that her Middle Credit Score of 620 was a key factor driving those increases. It was a moment of clarity that reshaped how she viewed credit. This was not about borrowing money; it was about the hidden costs of financial invisibility.

Instead of accepting higher premiums as unavoidable, Rebecca acted. She reviewed her credit reports line by line, identifying outdated charge-offs that should no longer have been reporting. She automated all payments to eliminate the risk of late fees and aggressively reduced her revolving balances to lower utilization.

Just as important, she began regularly monitoring her credit, catching issues before they could compound.

Within nine months, Rebecca's Middle Credit Score climbed into the low 700s. When her insurance renewed, the impact was immediate, a nearly 20% reduction across her policies. The savings were not just financial; they restored her sense of control. Rebecca learned that credit awareness does not just unlock loans, it protects cash flow, reduces stress, and strengthens everyday financial stability.

From My Client Files - Example 66 (Chapter 8): Nathan's Credit Turnaround and Career Opportunity

Nathan was weeks away from securing his first significant career opportunity when an unexpected obstacle surfaced. During the background check process, duplicate accounts and an old charge-off long since settled pulled his Middle Credit Score down to 580. What frustrated him most was not the number itself, but the realization that unresolved credit issues could cost him a job he had already earned through merit.

Rather than reacting emotionally, Nathan approached the situation methodically. He pulled his reports, disputed inaccurate information, and began rebuilding a positive history immediately. He used a secured credit card responsibly, tracked his progress in a journal, and negotiated deletions where possible. Every step was documented, every improvement measured.

Within five months, Nathan's Middle Credit Score reached 700. When the employer reran his credit as part of onboarding, the concern was gone. He secured the position and entered the workforce with a deeper understanding of how credit impacts professional opportunities. Nathan's story reinforces a critical truth: credit health extends beyond finances it; influences trust, responsibility, and access in ways many people never anticipate.

From My Client Files - Example 67 (Chapter 8): Disciplined Savings and Credit Growth Strategy

---

Megan wanted to buy her first home but felt trapped between saving for a down payment and improving her Middle Credit Score, which was stuck near 600. Instead of trying to fix everything at once, she adopted a disciplined, written approach. She began journaling weekly, tracking spending, setting modest savings goals, and documenting every credit improvement milestone. Her journal became both a plan and a motivator.

She focused on lowering credit card balances, steadily reducing utilization, and learning to budget realistically rather than restrictively. Visual reminders, such as photos, timelines, and progress notes, kept her focused when motivation dipped. Over time, her habits shifted from reactive to intentional.

Eighteen months later, Megan had saved several thousand dollars and raised her Middle Credit Score into the high 600s. She qualified for an FHA loan and purchased her first home. Income increases, or shortcuts, did not drive her success; it was driven by consistency, education, and self-accountability. Megan's journey proves that structure transforms intention into results.

Section 1: Lessons That Emerge from Real-Life Credit Transformation

When viewed collectively, these stories reveal patterns that are far more important than individual outcomes. Each person began at a different place, faced unique obstacles, and pursued other goals, yet the same principles surfaced repeatedly. Awareness preceded action. Structure replaced emotion. Consistency outperformed urgency. Credit improvement was not accidental; it was engineered.

These individuals did not rely on luck or external rescue. They took ownership of their financial narrative, learned how credit truly works, and aligned daily habits with long-term outcomes. The lesson is not that credit improvement is easy, but that it is predictable when approached with knowledge and discipline.

Key Actions Reinforced by These Stories

1. Reviewing credit reports regularly and correcting inaccuracies
2. Reducing credit utilization through intentional balance management
3. Establishing consistent, on-time payment behavior
4. Using journaling or documentation to maintain focus and accountability
5. Understanding how credit impacts areas beyond borrowing, including insurance, employment, and housing

These actions are simple, but their impact compounds over time when applied consistently.

Section 2: Applying These Lessons to Your Own Financial Journey

Success stories are only valuable if they lead to action. The purpose of this chapter is not inspiration alone, but application. Every reader can identify with at least one of these scenarios, whether it's rebuilding after hardship, protecting against fraud, or preparing for a significant milestone. The next step is to translate insight into behavior.

Credit improvement does not require perfection. It requires awareness, patience, and structure. When you understand how your Middle Credit Score is influenced and take deliberate steps to manage it, you regain control over outcomes that once felt uncertain.

5 Actionable Steps for Your Financial Journey You Can Take Now

1. Pull and review all three credit reports with accuracy in mind.
2. Identify the single factor having the most significant negative impact on your Middle Credit Score.
3. Create a written plan focused on one improvement area at a time.
4. Track progress monthly using a journal or structured system.
5. Align credit decisions with long-term goals rather than short-term convenience.

These steps create momentum. Momentum creates confidence. Confidence creates leverage.

Chapter 8 Closing: Turning Proof into a Personal Framework

The stories in this chapter exist for one reason: to remove doubt. Doubt that improvement is possible. Doubt that past mistakes permanently define you. Doubt that credit is something only experts or high earners can control. Every individual you read about faced a fundamental credit-related constraint, and every outcome changed once awareness, structure, and consistency replaced avoidance.

What these stories make clear is that credit improvement is not random, and it is not reserved for the fortunate. It follows patterns: accuracy matters, utilization matters, and timing issues in documentation. Most importantly, repeated behavior matters more than intensity or urgency. Each success you saw was built through ordinary actions executed consistently.

Your Middle Credit Score is not a verdict on who you are. It is feedback on what you are doing. When you respond to that feedback intentionally, the system reacts predictably. The lesson of this chapter is not inspiration, it is confirmation. The same principles apply regardless of the starting point when applied with discipline.

The One Action Framework

The "Credit Awareness Proof" Plan (30 / 60 / 90 Days)

Days 1–30: Establish Accuracy and Awareness
Pull all three credit reports and verify accuracy across every account, balance, and status. Identify errors, outdated items,

duplicates, or unfamiliar accounts. Begin documenting everything you review so progress is visible and measurable.

Days 31–60: Control the Levers That Actually Move Outcomes

Lower revolving utilization intentionally, even if balances are temporary. Automate payments to protect payment history. Avoid new inquiries and unnecessary credit activity. Focus on stability, not movement.

Days 61–90: Protect Progress and Lock in Consistency

Follow up on disputes and corrections. Introduce safeguards such as alerts, credit freezes when appropriate, and mid-cycle payments during high-spend periods. Credit should feel boring, predictable, and controlled; that's when it's working.
This is how results compound.

Chapter 8 Final Takeaways

- Credit improvement follows predictable patterns, not luck
- Awareness always precedes sustainable change
- Accuracy and utilization are foundational levers
- Documentation and tracking reinforce accountability
- Credit impacts far more than borrowing, including insurance, employment, and housing
- Consistency outperforms urgency every time
- Financial setbacks do not define financial futures
- Your Middle Credit Score is feedback, not identity
- Stability is built through repeatable systems
- What works for others can work for you when applied intentionally

Empowering the Next Generation with Financial Literacy

Turning Knowledge into Legacy

The truth is that financial literacy is not something most people are ever formally taught; they learn it through pain, setbacks, and expensive mistakes. I have seen it for decades. A person can be intelligent, hardworking, and full of potential, and still get trapped because they were never taught how money and credit work, or how one careless decision can ripple into years of consequences. What is even harder to watch is when those same patterns repeat from one generation to the next, not because families do not care, but because nobody ever pulled them aside early enough to show them the blueprint.

This chapter is about breaking that cycle. Not with theory. Not with "one day you should…" advice. But with practical, real-world financial education that starts early and grows with a child as they become a teenager, then an adult, then a parent themselves. It is about teaching young people what most adults wish someone would have taught them: how to budget without fear, how to save with purpose, how to use credit like a tool, and how to protect their Middle Credit Score® before life ever requires them to rely on it.

Because the next generation is entering a world that moves faster, costs more, and punishes ignorance harder than ever. One swipe, one missed payment, one ignored bill, or one identity theft event can derail a young adult's finances before they even get a real chance to stabilize. Yet the opposite is also true: when a young person understands financial basics early, builds credit correctly, learns to protect their information, and gets comfortable tracking money, their confidence changes. Their decisions change. Their outcomes change.

I want this chapter to feel like a handoff. Like I am sitting across the table from a parent, an aunt, a mentor, a coach, or a young adult, and I'm saying: Here is how you build the foundation. Here is how you protect it. Here is how you turn knowledge into a legacy, because what you teach now does not just help them "get by." It prepares them to qualify for loans, negotiate, avoid bad debt, build wealth, and live with financial options rather than financial stress.

That is what empowerment really looks like.

Section 1: The Foundation of Financial Literacy: The Role of Early Education

Building a foundation in financial literacy begins with understanding the basics: earning, spending, saving, and managing credit. It is not about becoming an expert overnight; it is about mastering the essentials that guide lifelong financial decisions. When young people grasp the significance of budgeting, credit management, and setting realistic goals, they establish a roadmap for economic success. Financial literacy is not just a class; it is a lifestyle that should evolve as they grow and face new challenges.

One of the most overlooked yet impactful areas of financial literacy is credit education. Many young adults graduate with little knowledge of how credit impacts everything from loan approvals to rental applications. Teaching them about the Middle Credit Score® early on ensures they understand the power of their credit behaviors and the opportunities strong credit can unlock. Tools like a credit journal and practical exercises, such as calculating interest rates or reviewing sample credit reports, make these concepts relatable and actionable.

When kids learn early, they do not fear money. They do not treat money like a mystery. They treat it like a system they can understand. Once a child believes they can understand something, they become less likely to avoid it and more likely to master it. That is the turning point. That is where habits become identity.

From My Client Files - Example 68 (Chapter 9): How Early Habits Built a 720 Middle Credit Score®

One of my most memorable experiences as a loan officer involved working with a family determined to teach their teenage son, Kevin, the value of financial literacy. Kevin's parents had experienced credit challenges early in their lives, which delayed their ability to purchase their first home. They wanted to ensure Kevin had the tools to avoid similar mistakes and build a strong foundation for his financial future.

We started by reviewing the family's credit reports together, using them as a real-world example to teach Kevin about credit utilization, payment history, and the importance of maintaining a healthy Middle Credit Score. Kevin began tracking his financial habits with a credit journal documenting his allowance, savings goals, and small expenditures. Inspired by his parents' guidance, he set his first goal: saving enough to contribute toward a family vacation. Along the way, he learned how budgeting and planning influence real decisions.

By the time Kevin entered college, he had opened a secured credit card and managed it responsibly by making small purchases and paying the balance in full each month. His understanding of financial literacy helped him build a Middle Credit Score of 720 before graduation, setting him up to secure his first car loan and later apply for his own mortgage.

Financial literacy starts at home, real-world examples make credit real, and journaling builds accountability. When young people set attainable goals and learn how credit works early, they don't just avoid mistakes; they gain access to opportunities.

Section 2: Credit Education Starts with the Middle Credit Score®

Understanding the Middle Credit Score is a vital part of teaching financial literacy to the next generation. It is not just about knowing the score; it is about grasping what it controls. For a young adult, this one number can determine whether they get approved for an apartment, how much they pay for a car, what terms they're offered on a loan, and in some cases even how employers or insurers evaluate them. That is why this conversation cannot wait until they are already applying for something important.

When you introduce the Middle Credit Score® early, you demystify the credit system. You remove the fear. You remove the confusion. And you give them a framework: payment history matters, utilization matters, time matters, and discipline matters. These are life principles disguised as credit principles. And when they understand that credit is not a lottery, but a predictable scoring model, they start to see how their daily decisions shape their future.

This is where empowerment becomes real. It is not "be careful with credit." It's "here is how the system works, and here is how you win."

From My Client Files - Example 69 (Chapter 9): Teaching Financial Responsibility

---

I worked with a single mother, Marie, who was determined to teach her teenage son, Ethan, financial responsibility before he left for college. Ethan was bright but had almost no understanding of how credit worked or how it could shape his future. Marie wanted him equipped before adulthood forced the lesson.

We created a plan: Ethan became an authorized user on Marie's card, and they used a journal to track spending and payments. He learned to treat credit like a responsibility, not a reward. By graduation, Ethan had a Middle Credit Score® of 720, strong enough to secure a low-interest car loan and begin adult life on a solid footing.

Start early, use parental guidance wisely, make it real with scenarios, and build independence gradually. The earlier a young adult understands the Middle Credit Score, the earlier they gain leverage in life.

Section 3: The Family's Role in Financial Education

Parents and guardians are the first teachers of financial behavior. Kids absorb more from what they see than what they are told. If they grow up watching bills go unpaid, credit get ignored, and budgeting get treated like a punishment, they carry that mindset forward. But if they grow up watching structured decision-making, thoughtful spending, and credit used responsibly, they inherit confidence rather than fear.

Financial education does not require families to be perfect. It requires families to be honest. You can teach more through transparency than through pretending everything is fine. A child can learn powerful lessons by observing how a family sets priorities, builds savings goals, and handles financial setbacks without panic. Those moments shape maturity.

The most effective family education is interactive. It is not a lecture. It is participation. Let them see how a budget is formed. Let them watch how savings accumulate. Let them understand why paying on time matters. Because when they can connect money decisions to outcomes, they become less impulsive and more intentional.

From My Client Files - Example 70 (Chapter 9): Household Budgeting Taught Life Lessons

---

I worked with the Martinez family, who wanted not only a home loan but also a plan to prepare their teenage son, Carlos, for adulthood. Instead of treating money as an adult-only topic, they involved him directly in household budgeting, showed him real expense categories, and explained how monthly decisions affected long-term outcomes. They added Carlos as an authorized user on a low-balance card that was paid in full each month, not to give him spending power, but to teach responsibility. They also set a family savings goal for a summer trip and assigned Carlos a portion of the budget to manage, making the process tangible instead of theoretical.

What mattered most was consistency. Carlos wasn't lectured; he was included. He learned how cash flow works, how trade-offs are made, and how discipline creates options. When unexpected expenses arose, the family discussed them openly, reinforcing that budgeting is not about restriction but about prioritization. Those conversations did more than teach math; they built confidence and accountability.

Within a year, Carlos understood credit and cash flow. At 18, he opened a secured card and used it correctly, keeping balances low and payments on time. By the time he graduated from college, his Middle Credit Score® was in the high 700s, and he secured a low-interest auto loan with confidence. The result was not luck; it was preparation in motion.

The lesson is simple but powerful: start early, involve kids in real budgeting, use authorized user accounts strategically, teach goal setting through action, and show through lived experience how strong credit leads to better life options.

Section 4: Teaching Credit Basics: Building Credit from Scratch

Building credit from scratch is one of the most essential life skills a young adult can learn because the credit system does not wait for them to "feel ready." The world assumes they know it. Landlords assume it. Lenders assume it. Sometimes employers assume it, and when a young adult has no credit, they often get treated like a risk, even if they have done nothing wrong.

The key is to show them that building credit is not about debt. It's about behavior. It's about using small amounts of credit in controlled ways to prove reliability over time. A secured credit card can be a powerful starting point. An authorized user account used responsibly can accelerate the building of a credit foundation. The goal is to teach them that credit is earned through consistent habits, not through big purchases.

When young adults understand how to build credit, they avoid the traps that destroy it: overspending, maxing out cards, and missing payments. That awareness protects them before they ever face the pressure of real-life decisions.

From My Client Files - Example 71 (Chapter 9): Building Credit History

---

Julian was turned down for his first apartment lease, not because of bad credit, but because he had no credit history. He was working, stable, and responsible, but the system could not measure him. We started him with a secured card for recurring bills, had him pay the balance in full each month and his parents added him as an authorized user to a long-standing low-balance account.

Six months later, Julian was approved for the apartment and had built a Middle Credit Score of around 680. Two years later, he was in the 740 range and qualified for a low-interest auto loan.

Credit history matters early, secured cards teach discipline, authorized user accounts can help when done right, reminders protect payment history, and early education creates long-term stability.

Section 5: Career-Ready Financial Habits

The moment a young adult begins earning real income, whether through college, internships, or their first job, financial habits either become a foundation or a fault line. This stage is where many people either learn structure or develop patterns that follow them for years. This is where budgeting shifts from theory to survival. Rent, gas, food, insurance, and student costs introduce pressure, and pressure reveals habits.

Career-ready habits start with controlling cash flow. Learning to manage checking and savings accounts properly, avoid overdrafts, set spending limits, and track expenses weekly builds confidence. When those habits are paired with credit awareness, a young adult becomes financially dangerous in the best way because they are hard to trap. They can qualify, negotiate, and avoid forced bad financial deals.

This is also where the mindset matters: credit is not "extra money." It is a tool that requires respect. If young adults learn that early, they avoid high-interest debt cycles before they ever begin.

From My Client Files - Example 72 (Chapter 9): Early Credit Awareness Helped College Graduate

I refinanced a family years ago and spent time teaching the parents how to involve their kids in savings and credit awareness. Nearly two decades later, their daughter, Megan, is now a college graduate with a strong financial profile. She had saved since childhood, maintained disciplined checking habits, and her parents had added her as an authorized user to build credit. Megan's Middle Credit Score was 760. She qualified for a competitive mortgage rate on her first condo, secured a low-interest auto loan, and landed her dream job, where her credit mattered during onboarding.

Early saving builds momentum, authorized user strategies build credit, disciplined spending drives qualification power, credit can affect career opportunities, and family modeling has a generational impact.

Section 6: Opening Checking and Savings Accounts as Kids and Teens

A checking account teaches responsibility in motion. A savings account teaches discipline over time. When kids and teens have both, they begin learning two essential lessons: how money moves and how money grows. These accounts create a real-world financial framework that's far more powerful than lectures. They turn money into something tangible and trackable.

For kids, savings accounts help them experience delayed gratification. For teens, checking accounts teach transaction awareness, budgeting, and consequences. A teen who learns how overdrafts happen becomes more careful. A teen who watches their savings grow becomes more confident. And when you connect these lessons to future goals, cars, college, and independence, they stop thinking of money as something that disappears and start thinking of money as something that can be directed.

This is also the perfect stage to introduce credit concepts without giving them full responsibility too soon. You can explain how credit works, why a Middle Credit Score matters, and how identity protection becomes part of financial maturity. This stage is not about fear. It's about preparation.

From My Client Files - Example 73 (Chapter 9): Savings Account Helped Educate Child

---

The Thompson family opened a savings account for their daughter Emily after she began asking questions about money. She deposited babysitting earnings, then opened a checking account when she started working part-time. Her parents added her as an authorized user and used the process to teach timely payments and low balances. By graduation, Emily had saved for a car down payment, built a healthy credit foundation, and developed confidence that shaped her future goals.

Early exposure builds lifelong habits, savings teaches delayed gratification, authorized-user strategies can build credit safely, real-world experiences prepare teens for adulthood, and family-led education fosters independence.

Section 7: Saving for College: Tools, Credit, and Financial Literacy

College preparation is often treated solely as a savings conversation. But it is bigger than savings; it is a planning conversation. College is a significant financial milestone, and without structure, families rely too heavily on debt, turning a degree into a burden rather than a launchpad. When financial literacy is built early, college becomes a planned milestone instead of a financial emergency.

This section matters because college expenses are not just tuition. They include housing, food, transportation, books, technology, and daily spending.

When teens understand budgeting before college begins, they avoid wasting thousands of dollars. And when families understand how credit affects borrowing costs, they can dramatically reduce long-term interest, especially for loans that depend on a parent's credit or require co-signing.

A strong Middle Credit Score can influence interest rates, approvals, and the total cost of borrowing. That's why teaching credit alongside saving is so powerful. It allows families to combine scholarships, savings, structured borrowing, and budgeting into a strategy that avoids regret later.

From My Client Files - Example 74 (Chapter 9): Education Without Being Buried in Debt

---

The Harper family wanted to fund their daughter Lisa's education without burying her in debt. They combined savings, scholarships, and strategic credit-building. Lisa worked part-time, tracked her savings, and her parents added her as an authorized user while teaching her responsible habits. By college time, Lisa had a Middle Credit Score around 720 and secured low-interest options while minimizing borrowing. After graduation, she had less debt than her peers, moved into her first apartment with confidence, and built an emergency fund early. Start early, credit impacts student borrowing costs, family involvement creates accountability, scholarships reduce dependency on debt, and financial literacy lasts beyond college.

Section 8: Empowering the Next Generation with Financial Literacy

Real change happens when young people can see how financial literacy applies to their lives. That's why these examples matter. They do not just teach concepts, they show outcomes. The purpose of every example is to give families a blueprint that can be repeated and scaled from childhood through adulthood.

From My Client Files - Example 75 (Chapter 9):
Knowledge with Savings Teach Discipline

The Johnson family taught their ten-year-old son, Ethan, to save by setting a specific goal: a bicycle. They opened a savings account and encouraged consistent deposits. Ethan experienced the pride of reaching his goal through discipline, and that pride turned saving into a habit rather than a punishment.

What mattered most was not the account or the dollar amount; it was the lesson embedded in the process. Ethan learned that money responds to behavior. That patience produces outcomes. That progress does not come from impulse, but from consistency. Years later, those same principles show up when kids begin using debit cards, managing allowances, or opening their first credit accounts. By tying savings to purpose instead of restriction, the Johnsons did not just help their son buy a bike; they gave him an early framework for how financial decisions work. And that framework, once learned young, becomes a reference point that protects future credit behavior before mistakes ever happen.

From My Client Files - Example 76 (Chapter 9):
Adding Authorized User Helped Educate

Vivian's parents introduced credit concepts before she turned eighteen by adding her as an authorized user on a long-standing, well-managed account. They did not do it to "boost" a score; they did it to teach behavior. Each month, they reviewed statements together and walked through utilization, statement balances, due dates, and how interest works when balances aren't paid in full. Credit was not treated as a secret or a shortcut; it was treated as a system that responds to habits.

What made the difference was structure. Vivian began journaling her spending, noting how purchases affected balances and how balances affected utilization. She learned that paying in full was not just "good," it was strategic. By the time she graduated, credit no longer felt intimidating or abstract. She understood cause and effect, because her education came before independence, she entered adulthood already fluent in the behaviors that protect a strong Middle Credit Score®, not because someone fixed mistakes later, but because those mistakes never needed to happen in the first place.

From My Client Files - Example 77 (Chapter 9): Saving for 529 Plan Taught Credit Lesson

---

Jake's parents did not treat saving for college and learning credit as two separate conversations. They treated them as one system. While contributing part-time income to a 529 plan, Jake was also introduced to credit in a controlled, intentional way. He used a secured credit card only for necessary expenses, gas, books, and small recurring costs, and paid the balance in full every month. The lesson was not about access. It was about responsibility, visibility, and follow-through.

What mattered most was the sequencing. Jake learned that saving came first, spending came second, and credit was never a substitute for either. Watching his 529 balance grow while simultaneously seeing how monthly payments affected his credit profile reinforced a critical truth early: credit works best when it supports a plan, not when it fills a gap. By the time he entered college, Jake did not just have savings and a clean credit file; he had confidence. He knew how to manage money without drifting into debt, because he had already practiced the discipline long before the stakes were high.

From My Client Files - Example 78 (Chapter 9): Budgeting Activity Taught Clear Lessons

---

The Martinez family understood something most parents miss financial literacy sticks when it's experienced, not explained. Instead of lecturing their daughters about money, they gave them responsibility. Each week, the girls were entrusted with managing a portion of the grocery budget. They had to plan meals, compare prices, make trade-offs, and stay within limits. Budgeting was not theoretical; it was tangible. Every decision had a consequence, and every choice mattered.

What made this powerful was the debrief. After each trip, the family talked through what worked, what did not, and why certain decisions led to better outcomes. The girls learned that budgeting is not about restriction, it is about prioritization. They saw firsthand how planning reduced stress, how impulse decisions narrowed options, and how discipline created flexibility. By the time credit entered the conversation later, budgeting already felt familiar. They were not afraid of limits because they understood that boundaries create control. That foundation made future financial decisions, including credit, far less intimidating and far more intentional.

From My Client Files - Example 79 (Chapter 9): Credit Built Intentionally Lasted

Marcus did not learn about credit in a classroom; he knew when access was denied. When he applied to rent his first apartment, the rejection surprised him. He had income, references, and a steady job, but the landlord viewed him as a risk because his credit file was thin and unproven. That moment reframed credit for him. It was not about borrowing money; it was about demonstrating reliability to people who did not know him personally.

Once Marcus understood how landlords evaluate risk, his approach changed. He did not rush to open multiple accounts or chase a fast score. Instead, he built credit intentionally. He was added as an authorized user on a well-managed account, monitored all three bureaus, and learned how utilization and payment timing affected his profile. He treated credit like a reputation; something built quietly through consistency rather than speed.

What stood out was not how fast his score improved, but how stable it became. By the time he applied for his next apartment, he did not need a co-signer or inflated deposits. The system now recognized what his habits already reflected. Marcus learned early what many people do not realize until much later: credit built with intention lasts longer, costs less, and opens doors without stress. That understanding did not just help him secure housing; it gave him the confidence to navigate every future financial decision that followed.

Chapter 9 Reflection: The Gift That Keeps Giving

If there is one thing I want you to walk away with from this chapter, it is this: financial literacy is one of the most powerful gifts you can give a child, a teen, or a young adult because it keeps giving for the rest of their life. When they understand money, they stop fearing it. When they know credit, they stop being controlled by it, and when they understand the Middle Credit Score® early, they stop walking into adulthood blind.

Financial empowerment does not start when someone is ready to buy a house. It begins when someone learns how to make small decisions with discipline and purpose long before the stakes are high. The young adult who knows to track spending, protect identity, keep utilization low, and pay on time is not just building a score; they are building a future. They are building trust, and that trust becomes leverage: lower costs, better approvals, and stronger options.

The real win is generational. When these principles are taught early, you do not just change one person's path; you change the family's trajectory. Money stops being a mystery. Credit stops being a trap. It becomes a tool, handled with intention.

Section 9: Protecting Young Credit Early, Avoiding the Mistakes That Follow Them for Years

One of the most dangerous myths young people believe is that credit mistakes are "small" when you are young. I have seen the opposite play out thousands of times. What happens at 18, 19, or 20 can shape what opportunities show up at 25, 30, and beyond, because credit does not just record what you did. It records who you were consistent enough to become. When a young adult racks up high balances, misses a payment, or ignores a collection notice, they usually are not trying to sabotage themselves. They simply do not understand that the credit system does not grade intentions; it grades behavior.

This is why protecting young credit early matters just as much as building it. If a young person creates a solid credit foundation but fails to learn the safeguards, they can lose in a single year what took them two or three years to earn. A missed payment, a maxed-out card, a few unnecessary inquiries, or a careless co-signer can drag down a Middle Credit Score fast. Once that happens, everything becomes more expensive: interest rates, deposits, insurance premiums, and even the "cost" of time, because opportunities require repairs rather than progress.

Protection also includes identity protection, because young adults are frequent targets. They are new to credit, they're applying for apartments, cars, and student programs, and they are sharing personal information in more places than they realize. One compromised account can create a mess they do not know how to clean up. What I want is for young people to understand this:

credit protection isn't paranoia. It is maturity. It is leadership over your future.

When you teach these safeguards early, you do not just prevent damage, you create a mindset. You make the habit of checking, tracking, and correcting. That is what separates people who stay stable from people who keep repeating financial emergencies.

7 Actionable Steps for Credit Safeguards Every Young Adult Needs (and Why They Matter)

1. **Teach the "One Rule" of On-Time Payments**
   - o Make it clear: one late payment can hurt a score for years.
   - o Set up autopay for minimum payments and calendar reminders for full payoff.

2. **Keep Credit Utilization Low from Day One**
   - o Explain utilization like this: the lower the balance, the stronger the trust signal.
   - o Target under **30%** but teach them the discipline of **10% or less** when possible.

3. **Limit Credit Applications and Hard Inquiries**
   - o Teach them to stop "shopping for credit cards" as entertainment.
   - o Apply only with purpose and space applications out strategically.

4. **Never Co-Sign Without a Written Plan**
   - o Co-signing is not kindness, it's shared liability.
   - o If co-signing ever happens, require a written repayment plan and proof of autopay.

5. **Monitor Credit Like You Monitor a Bank Account**
    o   Review credit reports for accuracy.
    o   Catch errors early before they become denials later.

6. **Protect Identity Like It's a Financial Asset (Because It Is)**
    o   Use strong passwords, avoid sharing personal data casually, and be cautious with public Wi-Fi.
    o   Teach credit freezes and fraud alerts as standard protection tools—not emergency actions.

7. **Use a Credit Journal to Track Behavior**
    o   Log due dates, balances, utilization, score changes, and goals.
    o   A journal creates accountability and keeps progress visible.

Section 10: Building a Legacy Mindset; Turning Financial Literacy into Generational Wealth

A young person who learns financial literacy is not just learning how to avoid debt. They are learning how to create options, and options are what separate survival from stability, and stability from wealth. This is where the conversation shifts from "how do we help them get started?" to "how do we help them build a legacy?" Because the goal is not simply to raise financially responsible adults, but to raise adults who understand systems such as credit, budgeting, and investing, and who pass that knowledge down, so the next generation starts even further ahead.

Generational wealth is not only about assets. It is about habits. It is about confidence. It is about knowing how to make decisions with clarity instead of fear. When young adults understand how the Middle Credit Score® works, they become more intentional about major life moves. They begin thinking about ownership earlier. They know that a strong credit profile reduces borrowing costs and improves the quality of opportunities. That alone can create a lifetime difference in net worth.

I have worked with families where the parents struggled for years but made one powerful decision: they taught their kids early, and the result was not just better credit scores. It was smarter choices, avoiding toxic debt, saving for down payments, negotiating interest rates, buying property sooner, and building stability with confidence. That is the legacy mindset. It does not require perfection. It requires intention, repetition, and leadership inside the household.

When a family treats financial literacy as a shared skill rather than a secret topic, they create unity. The next generation stops guessing. They stop learning through mistakes. They start learning through strategy, and strategy changes outcomes.

7 Actionable Steps for How to Build a Legacy Mindset in the Next Generation

1. **Make Financial Literacy a Household Standard**
   - Talk about money with calm structure, not stress.
   - Normalize budgeting, saving, and credit awareness as regular life skills.

2. **Teach Goals in Time Frames**
   - Short-term: emergency fund, small savings goals
   - Mid-term: car purchase, college planning, credit building
   - Long-term: homeownership, business ownership, retirement investing

3. **Connect the Middle Credit Score to Real Opportunities**
   - Show them the difference between high-interest and low-interest borrowing.
   - Explain how credit influences housing, insurance, and long-term costs.

4. **Introduce Ownership Thinking Early**
   - Teach the difference between paying for convenience vs. paying for assets.
   - Explain how ownership, especially real estate, often becomes a wealth-building lever.

5. **Create a "First Credit Wins" Plan**
   - A secured card or authorized user strategy used responsibly.
   - Automatic payments, low utilization, and periodic monitoring.

6. **Teach Investment Thinking as a Natural Next Step**
   - Start with basic concepts: compounding, retirement accounts, and consistent contributions.
   - Emphasize that wealth often comes from time + consistency, not luck.

7. **Build Family Accountability**
    o Use a journal or monthly family check-in:
        ▪ savings progress
        ▪ spending awareness
        ▪ credit habits
        ▪ goals and adjustments

Chapter 9 Closing: Teaching Credit is How You Break the Cycle

I have watched this pattern repeat for decades: people struggle with credit, not because they are irresponsible, but because no one ever taught them how the system works. What is passed down is fear, misinformation, and avoidance, not understanding. When credit is misunderstood, it quietly becomes a generational tax.

This chapter was not about perfection. It was about awareness. Because once you understand credit, you do not just improve your own outcomes, you change the conversations in your household. You stop normalizing late payments, maxed-out cards, and financial stress as "just how life is." You replace silence with clarity, and confusion with structure.

The most powerful financial move you can make is not raising your score; it is teaching the next generation how not to lose it. When knowledge replaces guesswork, progress becomes repeatable, and repeatable progress is how cycles break.

The One Action Framework

The "Generational Credit Awareness" Plan (30 / 60 / 90 Days)

Days 1–30: Create Awareness and Language

Choose one financial skill to teach weekly (budgeting, saving, credit basics). Open or review a checking and savings account plan for your child/teen. Introduce the Middle Credit Score concept in plain language and begin a simple money journal to track spending, saving, and goals.

Days 31–60: Build Structure, Habits, and Guardrails

Review your own credit habits and explain them out loud to a spouse, child, or family member. Pull credit reports together if appropriate. Introduce the idea that credit is not good or bad; it is a tool with rules. Create a family budgeting routine (weekly or biweekly check-in). Set savings goals in time frames (short, mid, long). Put safeguards in place: autopay minimums, reminders, and basic identity protection. If age-appropriate, begin a responsible credit-building strategy (e.g., an authorized user or a secured card) with clear rules and accountability.

Days 61–90: Turn Knowledge into a Lifestyle and a Legacy

Demonstrate on-time payments, intentional spending, and awareness of utilization. Show how balances affect scores. Make credit conversations normal instead of secretive while practicing real-world scenarios: renting, car purchasing, and credit decision-making. Review progress monthly using the journal and adjust goals. Teach the "non-negotiables" (on-time payments, low utilization, limited inquiries, no co-signing without a plan).

Connect strong credit to ownership thinking and long-term wealth building, so financial literacy becomes an identity, not a one-time lesson.

Chapter 9 Final Takeaways

• Financial literacy is learned best early, before adulthood forces expensive lessons
• The Middle Credit Score should be taught as a life tool, not a last-minute surprise
• Habits beat motivation: budgeting, saving, and credit awareness must become routine
• Credit protection matters as much as credit building, especially for young adults
• When families teach money openly and consistently, they build generational leverage

.

Decoding Tri-Merge Credit Reports and the FICO® Scoring System

How Lenders Interpret Your Credit Data

For most consumers, credit is something they *feel* more than they understand. They think the stress comes from a score dropping unexpectedly. They feel frustrated by being told they don't qualify, even though they have been making payments. They think the confusion occurs when one credit monitoring app shows one number and a lender shows another. Over the years, I have learned that the biggest problem is not that people are careless; it is that they were never taught how the system truly evaluates them.

That system is built on two core tools: the **Tri-Merge credit report** and the **FICO® scoring system**. These two components work together to determine how lenders view risk, how they price loans, and whether you are seen as a "safe" borrower or a "question mark." If you have ever wondered why two people with similar incomes can get wildly different interest rates, it often comes back to what the Tri-Merge report reveals and what the FICO® model interprets from it.

A **Tri-Merge credit report** is a single consolidated report that pulls data from the three major credit bureaus, **Experian, Equifax, and TransUnion,** and displays it together. That matters because credit reporting is not perfectly consistent across bureaus. One bureau may show an account as current while another shows it as delinquent. One bureau may list an old balance that was paid off months ago. Another bureau might be missing an account entirely, and those inconsistencies can lower the one score that most lenders care about most: your **Middle Credit Score®**.

The **FICO® scoring system** is the scoring engine that turns your credit behavior into a number. But here's where consumers get tripped up: FICO® isn't just one score. There are multiple FICO® versions and multiple industry-specific variations. Mortgage lenders often rely on older, more conservative models, while other lenders may reference more modern models. And with newer models like **FICO® 10 and FICO® 10T**, the system is increasingly focused on your behavior over time rather than just snapshots.

That evolution matters because the credit world is shifting toward what I call "pattern recognition." If you keep high balances on your revolving accounts month after month, even if you pay on time, trended data can interpret that as risk. If you steadily reduce balances over time, it can be interpreted as a sign of stability. In other words, your daily habits become part of your score story in a much more visible way than they used to be.

This chapter is designed to make you fluent, not in credit jargon but in the real-life mechanics that determine your approvals, your rates, your fees, and your opportunities. When you understand how Tri-Merge reports are built, how FICO® models score you, and why lenders lean on the Middle Credit Score, you stop guessing. You stop hoping. You start managing your credit with precision.

One of the most essential distinctions a consumer can learn is this: **the credit world you see is not the credit world lenders see.** Credit monitoring apps are designed to keep you engaged, not to prepare you for underwriting. They show simplified scores, limited data, and generalized advice because that is what works for consumers, not because it is what lenders rely on. This disconnect is the root of most credit-related frustration.

Lenders do not operate from snapshots. They operate from patterns. They do not ask, "Is this score high?" They ask, "Is this borrower stable?" Stability shows up in consistency across bureaus, disciplined utilization behavior, clean reporting, and predictable trends over time. A consumer-facing score might rise or fall based on short-term activity, but a lender is trained to look past that noise and assess whether the credit profile tells a reliable story.

This is why so many borrowers feel blindsided. They are monitoring a score that is not being used, optimizing behaviors that do not move pricing, and reacting emotionally to changes that do not matter, or worse, ignoring issues that do. When a lender pulls a Tri-Merge report using a specific FICO® model, the decision is already being framed by factors the consumer may never have seen clearly before. That is not deception; it is a difference in purpose.

Understanding this difference changes everything. It shifts you from consumer mode to borrower mode. Instead of asking, "Why did my score drop?" you start asking, "What changed in my profile that a lender would flag?" Instead of chasing points, you focus on accuracy, utilization control, and trend stability. That's the shift from confusion to strategy.

This chapter exists to close that gap, not by teaching you to game the system, but by teaching you to **see what lenders see**. When your understanding matches their evaluation method, your results stop feeling random. Credit becomes predictable. And predictability is where leverage lives.

Section 1: Tri-Merge Credit Reports: A Comprehensive Look at Your Financial Profile

A Tri-Merge credit report is the lender's complete baseline view of your financial identity. It combines your credit data from Experian, Equifax, and TransUnion into a single document so the lender can compare what each bureau reports simultaneously.

For a consumer, that means the Tri-Merge report often exposes what credit apps do not clearly show: bureau-to-bureau inconsistencies that can change your loan outcome.

This matters because the credit bureaus do not operate as a single, synchronized system. Each bureau receives data from creditors at slightly different times. Some lenders report to all three bureaus, while others report to only one or two. Some accounts update monthly, while others update irregularly, and when disputes happen, one bureau might correct an item quickly while another takes longer or does not correct it at all. That is how consumers end up with "split reality," where their credit file is clean on one bureau and messy on another.

The Tri-Merge report also matters because it often becomes the foundation for how your Middle Credit Score® is selected. In mortgage lending, **especially**, lenders typically pull three scores: one from each bureau, using a specific FICO® model. They then rely on the middle score, the median of the three. That means one incorrect collection, one misreported late payment, or one outdated balance can drag the middle score down enough to change your pricing tier.

When you understand the Tri-Merge report, you stop focusing only on the score and start focusing on what produces the score. You start thinking like a lender: "What does this profile tell me about stability?" "Is the data consistent?" "Are there red flags?" Once you do that, you are no longer at the mercy of the system; you are in control of it.

5 Actionable Steps to Navigate Tri-Merge Credit Reports (Steps List)

1. **Request Your Tri-Merge Report Early**
   - Ask your lender for a Tri-Merge report before major credit decisions, especially before a mortgage or refinance.

2. **Compare All Three Bureau Columns**
   - Look for accounts that appear on one bureau, but not another.
   - Flag any account with mismatched balances, statuses, or dates.

3. **Verify Account Status Accuracy**
   - Confirm that closed accounts show as closed, paid accounts show as paid, and discharged debts show as discharged when applicable.

4. **Identify the "Score-Draggers"**
   - High utilization, derogatory items, late payments, collections, and frequent inquiries.
   - Determine which bureau is pulling the middle score down.

5. **Document Discrepancies Immediately**
   - Create a simple dispute log: bureau, account name, issue, documentation, date submitted, and follow-up date.

The Impact of a Tri-Merge Credit Report

From My Client Files - Example 80 (Chapter 10): Tri-Merge Credit Report Produced Different Outcomes

I remember working with James, a young professional preparing to buy his first home. He came in confident because he had been monitoring his credit and believed his score was strong enough to qualify for a solid rate. But when his lender pulled the Tri-Merge report, we saw something that happens more often than people realize: two bureaus told one story, while the third said another.

Experian and Equifax showed James with a stable payment history and a score that supported his home loan goal. TransUnion, however, still reflected an old collection account that had been resolved. That single outdated item didn't just lower a score; it shifted his loan options into a less favorable category. It would have cost him more every month, and significantly more over the life of the mortgage.

*We immediately gathered his proof of payment and filed a dispute with TransUnion. At the same time, I communicated clearly with the lender, so they understood what we were correcting and why. Within about 30 days, the item was removed, his scores aligned, and his **Middle Credit Score®** rebounded to where it should have been in the first place. James didn't have a credit problem; he had a reporting problem. Once he saw that distinction, he became far more confident and proactive moving forward.*

Takeaways

1. *One bureau error can impact your Middle Credit Score even when the other two are strong.*
2. *Tri-Merge reports reveal discrepancies that most apps do not explain clearly.*

3. *Documentation is the key to winning disputes quickly.*

4. *Aligning bureau data can improve pricing tiers, not just approvals.*

5. *The earlier you review the Tri-Merge report, the more control you have.*

Section 2: Understanding FICO® Scoring Models: Why Your "Score" Is Not Just One Score

Most consumers are told to "raise your FICO® score," as if there is one universal number that follows you everywhere. In reality, FICO® is a scoring system with multiple versions and multiple variations designed for different industries. A credit card issuer may view your risk differently from a mortgage lender. An auto lender may prioritize different data patterns than a personal loan lender. That is why consumers can be confused when a score they see online does not match what a lender pulls.

Mortgage lending is a perfect example. Many mortgage lenders rely on older, conservative FICO® models that weigh derogatory items and payment history differently than newer versions. That means the way your profile is scored for a mortgage may not be identical to the way it's scored for a credit card. Newer models, such as **FICO® 10 and FICO® 10T,** may incorporate trended data, which evaluates how your balances and usage patterns behave over time.

Trended data changes the game. It rewards consistency and penalizes repeated high utilization patterns, even when payments are made on time. In other words, the scoring system is increasingly designed to distinguish between someone who uses credit responsibly over time and someone who constantly leans on revolving debt. That is why modern scoring rewards discipline, not perfection, but consistency.

The important takeaway is this: you don't need to chase every scoring model. You need habits that score well under all of them. Those habits are timeless: on-time payments, low utilization, clean reporting, smart borrowing, and stable behavior before major credit events.

5 Actionable Steps to Understand and Work with FICO® Models (Steps List)

1. **Know Which Lending Goal You're Preparing For**
    o Mortgage, auto, credit card, and personal loans each may use different FICO® versions.

2. **Ask the Right Question**
    o Instead of "What is my score?" ask: "Which FICO® model is being used for this decision?"

3. **Protect Your Payment History Above All**
    o Late payments are devastating across nearly every scoring model.

4. **Lower Utilization Consistently**
    o Keep balances below 30% and aim for 10% or less for the best scoring outcomes.

5. **Avoid "Score Noise" Before Major Moves**
    o Limit inquiries and avoid opening new accounts in the months leading up to a mortgage.

From My Client Files - Example 81 (Chapter 10): Navigating FICO® Updates and the Middle Credit Score

I worked with Jason and Mia, a young couple excited about buying their first home. Jason was frustrated because the score he had been watching did not match what the lender pulled. He felt blindsided, as if the system were changing the rules in the middle of the game. But once we walked through it, the truth was simple: different models weigh risk differently, and mortgage lending often uses versions consumers are not monitoring.

We shifted focus away from the "number shock" and toward what truly mattered, strengthening the profile that drives the Middle Credit Score under the lender's model. We reviewed their Tri-Merge report, identified what was dragging down one bureau, and implemented a strategy focused on utilization control, correction of reporting issues, and stable habits. Three months later, their Middle Credit Score® rose into a stronger tier even under the conservative model, allowing them to lock in better terms and reduce long-term costs.

They did not win by chasing a magical score. They won by understanding what lenders measure and making sure their profile reflected stability across all three bureaus.

Takeaways

1. *Not all lenders use the same FICO® model; mortgage models can be more conservative.*
2. *Your Middle Credit Score is often the decision score for pricing and approval.*
3. *Tri-Merge review reveals where one bureau is harming the middle score.*
4. *Utilization and reporting accuracy are fast-impact areas when time matters.*
5. *Strong habits outperform "score tricks" across all models.*

Section 3: Strategies for Optimizing Your Score Under New Models

Optimizing your score in today's environment requires you to think in two directions at once: **accuracy** and **trend**. Accuracy means your Tri-Merge data is correct across all three bureaus. Trend means your credit behavior looks stable over time, especially with models that track patterns. When both are strong, your Middle Credit Score becomes less volatile and far more powerful.

Accuracy is where many consumers miss easy wins. A duplicate account, an outdated balance, a misreported status, or an old item that should have been updated can create unnecessary score drag. Trend is where long-term strength is built. Consistently lowering balances, avoiding revolving-debt spikes, keeping utilization low month after month, and protecting payment history create a profile lenders trust.

This is the shift I want you to embrace: stop treating credit like something you check occasionally, and start treating it like something you manage intentionally, especially when you know you will be applying for a significant loan. The goal is not to be perfect. The goal is to be consistent, accurate, and stable.

5 Actionable Steps for Optimizing Under New FICO® Models (Steps List)

1. **Audit Tri-Merge Consistency**
   - o Identify items that don't match across bureaus and correct them

2. **Manage Utilization Like a Professional**
   - Keep overall utilization under 30%, ideally under 10%
   - Avoid allowing a single card to spike, even if others are low

3. **Pay Down Balances in a "Trending" Pattern**
   - Create a steady downward movement in revolving balances from month to month
   - Consider mid-cycle payments if you tend to carry high balances temporarily

4. **Reduce Debt Without Creating New Risk**
   - Avoid opening new accounts while optimizing for major lending decisions

5. **Give Yourself a Time Buffer**
   - Start these strategies 3–6 months before a mortgage if possible

Section 4: Credit Report Mastery: How to Read Your Tri-Merge Like a Lender

If there is one skill that separates a consumer who "hopes" for approval from a consumer who "controls" the outcome, it's this: learning to read your Tri-Merge report like a lender reads it. Lenders do not just look at the score. They look at the story. They scan for risk indicators, inconsistencies, and behaviors that suggest instability even when the score seems decent. That is why two borrowers with similar scores can get different outcomes depending on what the Tri-Merge reveals.

A lender is silently asking questions as they read your file: Are the accounts reporting consistently? Are there recent delinquencies? Are balances trending up or down? Are there unresolved collections? Does the borrower appear to be leaning heavily on revolving credit? Are there disputed remarks that might pause underwriting? These are not emotional questions. They are risk questions, and when you learn to see what they see, your actions become far more effective.

Tri-Merge mastery also protects you from surprises. It prevents the "I did not know that was still there" moment. It prevents the "I paid that off, but it did not update" problem, which can lead to frustration when you discover that one bureau is dragging your Middle Credit Score down, while the other two are strong.

7 Actionable Steps for The Lender-Style Tri-Merge Review Checklist

1. **Confirm Your Personal Information**
   - Name variations, addresses, employers, and identifying details should be accurate and consistent.

2. **Scan for Derogatory Items First**
   - Collections, charge-offs, late payments, bankruptcies, judgments.
   - Identify what is active, resolved, and outdated.

3. **Check Each Tradeline for Status Accuracy**
   - Open/closed, paid/unpaid, current/late, correct limits and balances.

4. **Audit Utilization by Card**
   - o Identify any disproportionately high card.
   - o One maxed-out card can lower your score even if the rest look fine.

5. **Compare Bureau-to-Bureau Reporting**
   - o If one bureau shows an error, treat it as a real threat to your middle score.

6. **Review Inquiries and Confirm They're Legit**
   - o Flag suspicious inquiries immediately and take protective steps.

7. **Document What You Find**
   - o Keep a credit log: bureau, item, issue, action taken, dates, status.

Section 5: The 30-Day Middle Credit Score Alignment Plan

Most people wait until they are ready to buy a home, refinance, or finance a car before they get serious about credit. That's like trying to train for a marathon the week before the race. If you want consistent approvals, strong pricing, and fewer surprises, you need a repeatable plan that improves accuracy and trend without panic.

This 30-day alignment plan is not a "hack." It is a short, structured system designed to clean up reporting issues, stabilize utilization, reinforce positive trends, and protect your Middle Credit Score from avoidable damage. It works because it focuses on what lenders measure. It prioritizes the fast-impact areas: errors, utilization, and stability.

If you repeat this type of rhythm quarterly, or even before major credit moves, you stop being reactive. You become prepared, and prepared borrowers do not just get approved; they get better terms.

7 Actionable Steps for Your 30-Day Credit Alignment Checklist

1. **Days 1–3: Pull Reports + Identify Inconsistencies**
   o Compare bureau columns and highlight mismatches
2. **Days 4–7: Dispute Clear Errors**
   o Duplicate accounts, outdated balances, and incorrect statuses
   o Submit documentation and log everything
3. **Days 8–14: Reduce High Utilization**
   o Attack the highest-utilization card first
   o Aim for overall utilization under 30%, with a stretch goal under 10%
4. **Days 15–18: Stabilize Payments**
   o Autopay minimums
   o Reminders for strategic paydowns
5. **Days 19–23: Pause New Credit Activity**
   o No new applications
   o No unnecessary account changes
6. **Days 24–27: Monitor Updates**
   o Ensure balances and dispute results are reflected across bureaus

7. **Days 28–30: Set Your Ongoing Routine**
   o Monthly: utilization and due date review
   o Quarterly: bureau comparison
   o Annually: full audit and goal reset

Chapter 10 Closing: Seeing What Lenders Actually See

Tri-Merge credit reports and FICO® scoring models exist to remove guesswork from lending decisions. They give lenders a consistent way to evaluate risk across three bureaus, multiple scoring systems, and years of borrower behavior. But for consumers, that same system often feels opaque until you understand how it really works.

This chapter was about clarity. Once you understand how the Tri-Merge report exposes inconsistencies, how FICO® models interpret patterns over time, and why the Middle Credit Score becomes the controlling number, you stop being surprised by outcomes. You stop relying on consumer-facing scores that do not drive pricing, and you start managing your credit the way lenders evaluate it.

Credit decisions are not emotional. They're systematic, and when you understand the system, you gain leverage. You can correct errors before they cost you money. You can stabilize behavior before it affects pricing, and you can approach major financial decisions prepared rather than reactively.

This is not about gaming the system. It is about understanding it well enough to protect yourself from unnecessary costs and to ensure your credit profile accurately reflects who you really are.

The One Action Framework

The "Tri-Merge & FICO® Alignment" Plan (30 / 60 / 90 Days)

Days 1–30: Establish Accuracy
Pull a full Tri-Merge credit report and compare bureau-by-bureau reporting. Identify mismatches, outdated balances, incorrect statuses, or unresolved derogatory items that could suppress the Middle Credit Score. Begin disputes with documentation and log every action.

Days 31–60: Stabilize Trends
Strategically lower revolving balances to improve utilization across all bureaus. Eliminate behaviors that create volatility, such as new inquiries, unnecessary account changes, or balance spikes. Allow corrected data to post and normalize across bureaus.

Days 61–90: Prepare for Decision-Grade Review
Maintain low utilization, flawless payment history, and zero unnecessary credit activity. Monitor updates for consistency and ensure your profile tells a clear, stable story. This is the phase where patience protects pricing and where disciplined borrowers gain an advantage.

Chapter 10 Final Takeaways

• Tri-Merge reports reveal bureau inconsistencies that directly affect loan pricing

• FICO® scoring is model-specific, and mortgage scores are often more conservative

• The Middle Credit Score is commonly the decision score lenders trust

• Accuracy and trend matter more than isolated score snapshots

• Understanding the system turns credit from confusion into control

11

Futureproofing Your Credit

Strategies for Long-Term Financial Health

Planning for the future starts with a mindset shift: credit is not just something you "use" when you need a loan, it's a reputation you build every month of your life. Over the years, I have watched people do everything right in the short term, only to get blindsided later because they never built a system that could withstand real life. And real life always shows up. A job change. A medical bill. A divorce. A recession. A broken transmission. A child heading to college. The question is not whether life will test your finances; the question is whether your credit profile has the structure to stay strong when it does.

That is what futureproofing is. It is not about obsessing over a number. It is about designing your financial life, so your **Middle Credit Score®** stays stable through change. Stability is what lenders reward. It keeps your rates lower, expands your options, and gives you leverage when opportunity appears. When your credit is stable, you can refinance when the opportunity appears. You can move when the right job appears. You can invest when the market shifts. You can say yes to a home when the timing is right, and you can do it without fear that one unexpected event will knock your score down and shut doors for months or years.

Futureproofing also means understanding that the credit world does not stand still. Scoring models evolve. Lenders tighten guidelines in uncertain markets. Technology changes how accounts are reported and monitored. The rules of risk change depending on the economy. The consumers who win in the long term are those who keep their fundamentals strong, stay proactive, and build buffers to prevent panic decisions. I have seen clients transform their lives by doing small things consistently, automating savings, keeping utilization low, disputing errors quickly, and building habits that hold up under pressure. Those are not flashy moves. They are durable moves, and durability is what creates long-term financial health.

This chapter will give you that durability. We are going to talk about building a safety net that protects your payment history. We are going to talk about diversifying the tools you rely on so one disruption does not knock you off balance. We are going to talk about adapting to economic shifts, staying ahead of technology, strengthening your financial literacy, and planning for significant life events before they arrive. The goal is simple: protect your

Middle Credit Score® as a long-term asset so it keeps working for you, not against you.

Section 1: Build a Financial Safety Net

A financial safety net is the foundation of long-term credit health because it protects the two most sensitive parts of your credit profile: **on-time payments** and **credit utilization**. When life hits, most people do not lose credit points because they suddenly become irresponsible. They lose points because their cash flow is disrupted and they start leaning on credit cards, miss due dates, or juggle bills in survival mode. A safety net prevents those "survival decisions" from causing permanent damage.

A real safety net is more than a savings account. It is a complete buffer system: emergency cash, a realistic budget, insurance coverage that prevents major financial leaks, and a plan for what you do if income drops. When you have that system, you are far less likely to carry high balances month after month, far less likely to miss a payment, and far more likely to handle emergencies with confidence. That confidence matters because it keeps you from using credit emotionally, opening accounts out of fear, and taking on high-interest debt. After all, when people feel trapped, they often use credit emotionally or ignore problems until they get worse.

Your Middle Credit Score benefits directly from a safety net because it keeps your report clean and your trends stable. Low utilization signals control. On-time payments signal reliability, and a steady credit pattern signals low risk. That is exactly what lenders want to see, especially when the economy tightens, and underwriting becomes less forgiving.

5 Actionable Steps to Build a Financial Safety Net

1. **Start an Emergency Fund**
   - o Save **3–6 months** of essential living expenses.
   - o Automate transfers to a high-yield savings account so the fund grows without willpower.

2. **Build a "Bills First" Budget**
   - o Separate needs from wants and prioritize essentials.
   - o Create a simple monthly baseline budget you can follow even during stress.

3. **Maintain Low Credit Utilization**
   - o Keep balances below **30%** of your limits and aim for **10% or less** when possible.
   - o Preserve available credit as a tool, not as a crutch.

4. **Reduce Financial Fragility**
   - o Identify one expense you can cut or renegotiate (subscriptions, insurance, phone plan).
   - o Redirect the difference into savings or debt reduction.

5. **Review Insurance Coverage**
   - o Confirm health, auto, renters/homeowners' coverage is adequate.
   - o The right coverage prevents emergencies from turning into long-term debt.

From My Client Files - Example 82 (Chapter 11): Minor Planning System Adjustments Changed Long-Term Outcome

I worked with a client, Karen, a single mother and a hardworking saver, who came to me after her Middle Credit Score dropped during an unexpected medical crisis. Her son needed surgery, and even though she did what many parents would do, she handled it; she did not have a strong enough safety net to absorb the impact. The bills came fast, her savings drained quickly, and credit cards became the bridge. Then the bridge became the burden. Utilization climbed, late payments occurred, and the score suffered.

What made Karen's situation painful was that her habits were not reckless; her system was incomplete. So, we built the system. We reviewed her reports, mapped out what was hurting her most, and stabilized cash flow first. She negotiated manageable payment terms with providers, consolidated high-interest revolving debt into a lower-interest option, and started rebuilding an emergency fund with small automatic deposits. That fund was not just money; it was protection. It prevented the next challenge from becoming another credit crisis.

Within a year, Karen rebuilt her Middle Credit Score from the low 600s back into a range that opened doors again. But more important than the score was what changed inside her: she stopped feeling like credit controlled her life. She felt prepared. And preparedness is what futureproofing looks like.

Takeaways
1. *A safety net prevents emergencies from becoming credit disasters.*
2. *Payment plans and negotiations can protect your score while you recover.*
3. *Consolidation can reduce pressure and utilization when done strategically.*
4. *Rebuilding is possible with consistent structure, not quick fixes.*
5. *An emergency fund is a credit-preservation tool, not just a savings goal.*

Section 2: Diversify Your Financial Tools

Relying on a single income stream or credit tool is like building a house on a single support beam. It might hold for a while, but when pressure hits, everything becomes unstable. Diversifying your financial tools means building flexibility into your life so you can adapt without damaging your credit. That flexibility could come from a healthy credit mix, multiple savings buckets, and income streams that prevent you from leaning too hard on revolving debt when things change.

From a credit standpoint, diversification is also about demonstrating capability. Lenders want to see that you can manage different types of obligations responsibly. Revolving credit shows how you handle ongoing access to credit. Installment loans show how you handle structured payments over time. A well-managed mix builds a stronger profile than relying on a single account type, because it signals maturity and stability.

Income diversification matters just as much. The fastest way to harm a Middle Credit Score is sudden income disruption combined with unplanned debt. When your income has more than one source, even if the second source is small, it increases resilience. Resilience protects payment history. It protects utilization, and it keeps you from making rushed decisions that create long-term damage.

5 Actionable Steps for Diversifying Your Financial Tools

1. **Maintain a Healthy Credit Mix**
   - Keep revolving accounts active and paid down.
   - Manage installment obligations responsibly if you have them.

2. **Create Multiple Financial "Buckets"**
   - Emergency fund, short-term savings, and planned expenses.
   - This prevents you from using credit for predictable life costs.

3. **Expand Income Streams**
   - Side work, freelance, consulting, or a small business adds stability.
   - Even a few hundred extra dollars per month reduces reliance on credit.

4. **Use Credit Strategically**
   - Keep accounts open (when appropriate) and avoid unnecessarily closing older lines.
   - Use credit for controlled spending; you can pay off, not for survival.

5. **Review Your Financial Toolkit Quarterly**
   - Ask: Do I have enough cushion? Enough flexibility? Too much reliance on one tool?
   - Adjust before stress forces the adjustment.

From My Client Files - Example 83 (Chapter 11): Rebuilding Financial Structure Requires Simple Processes

I once worked with a client named Jessie, a freelance designer who had an excellent Middle Credit Score but a fragile setup. Most of his income came from one major client. On paper, everything looked great until the client paused projects indefinitely. Suddenly, Jessie was covering expenses with credit cards, burning through savings, and watching utilization climb month after month. His score did not drop because he was irresponsible. It fell because its structure was not diversified enough to absorb the shock.

We rebuilt his foundation in two directions at once: lower the pressure now and reduce vulnerability moving forward. He consolidated high-interest revolving balances into a more manageable structure, then shifted his income strategy by adding multiple smaller clients and building a digital product he could sell consistently. His credit recovered, but more importantly, his life became less fragile. He was not depending on any one account, client, or financial "lane" anymore.

Takeaways

1. *A strong score can still sit on a fragile financial foundation.*
2. *Income diversification protects utilization and payment stability.*
3. *Consolidation can help when revolving debt becomes a pressure point.*
4. *A credit profile is strongest when supported by flexible cash flow.*
5. *Futureproofing is building options before you need them.*

Section 3: Adapt to Economic Changes

Economic shifts do not just affect Wall Street; they affect loan approvals, underwriting strictness, credit limits, interest rates, and the availability of financing. In strong markets, lenders compete, and approvals are easier. In uncertain markets, guidelines tighten, rates rise, and lenders become more conservative. If you are not prepared, you can find yourself paying more for the same loan or being denied when you thought you were ready.

Adapting to economic change means staying aware and staying ready. When rates drop, strong credit lets you refinance quickly. When rates rise, strong credit softens the impact because you still qualify for better terms. When lenders tighten, stable income and low utilization become even more critical. In other words, the economy may change, but the fundamentals that protect your Middle Credit Score® stay the same: discipline, low balances, timely payments, and planning.

The goal isn't to predict every shift. The goal is to build a credit and financial profile that performs well in any environment. That's futureproofing. It's resilience over prediction.

5 Actionable Steps for Adapting to Economic Changes

1. **Monitor Interest Rate Trends**
   o Stay aware of primary rate cycles and lending shifts.
   o Knowledge helps you time refinances and avoid unnecessary borrowing.

2. **Keep Debt-to-Income (DTI) Manageable**
   o Avoid overextending even when credit is available.
   o Lower DTI makes you stronger when lenders tighten lending standards.

3. **Prioritize High-Interest Debt Reduction**
   o Pay down revolving balances aggressively when possible.
   o High interest and high utilization are a double hit.

4. **Lock Stability When It's Available**
   o Fixed-rate structures can protect you from volatile rate environments.
   o Stability supports long-term planning.

5. **Strengthen Relationships with Financial Institutions**
   o A strong relationship and history can improve access and options.
   o This matters most when credit becomes harder to get.

From My Client Files - Example 84 (Chapter 11): Financial Stability Increased the Middle Credit Score®

I worked with Michelle as she prepared for her first home purchase. She had income stability, but her Middle Credit Score was hovering just below the tier that would get her the best mortgage pricing. The economy was shifting, and underwriting was tightening. That meant she didn't have the luxury of "eventually." She needed to build strength now without taking any risks.

We focused on the fundamentals that always matter: accuracy, utilization, and stability. She used monitoring tools to identify a reporting issue, corrected an error that had been dragging down one bureau, and then built a simple routine to consistently reduce balances. When rates and guidelines shifted, she was ready. She did not just qualify; she qualified in a stronger tier. That preparedness gave her better terms and a smoother approval process.

Takeaways
   1. Economic shifts punish weak credit profiles and reward stable ones.

2. *The best time to prepare is before you need financing.*
3. *Improvements in accuracy and utilization can move you into better pricing tiers.*
4. *Tight markets require cleaner profiles and more substantial buffers.*
5. *Stability becomes leverage when guidelines tighten.*

Section 4: Stay Ahead of Technological Advancements

Technology is reshaping credit management in two ways at once: it is giving consumers better tools and creating new risks. Credit monitoring is faster than ever allowing disputes to be initiated more easily, payments to be automated, and for trends to be tracked. But identity theft, data breaches, and digital fraud are also more common, and one fraud event can create months of stress if it hits your credit file.

Staying ahead does not mean chasing every new fintech trend. It means using technology intentionally: automated payments to protect your history, monitoring to spot errors early, strong cybersecurity to prevent fraud, and innovative tools that support consistent habits. The consumer who future-proofs their credit is not the one with the most apps; it's the one with the best system.

5 Actionable Steps to Stay Ahead of Technology

1. **Use Credit Monitoring with Purpose**
   o Track changes, alerts, and bureau differences.
   o Use the information to act, not just observe.

2. **Automate What Matters**
   o Set autopay minimums and reminders for strategic paydowns.

o   Automation protects you during busy or stressful months.

3. **Prioritize Cybersecurity**
   o   Strong passwords, two-factor authentication, and account alerts.
   o   Prevention is easier than cleanup.

4. **Evaluate Fintech Tools Carefully**
   o   Rent reporting, budgeting platforms, and alternative credit builders.
   o   Use tools that align with your goals and don't add risk.

5. **Create a Digital Financial Routine**
   o   Weekly quick check, monthly deeper review, quarterly strategy reset.
   o   Routine beats randomness every time.

Section 5: Cultivate Financial Literacy

Financial literacy is the skill that makes everything else in this chapter sustainable. Without it, people build credit accidentally sometimes in the right direction, sometimes in the wrong direction, and they do not realize what is happening until the score drops. With literacy, you understand what your actions are doing, why they matter, and how to adjust before problems grow.

The truth is that the credit system rewards the informed consumer. When you understand utilization, reporting cycles, disputes, budgeting, and lender expectations, you stop being intimidated. You ask better questions. You plan earlier. You negotiate from strength, while you teach your family the same skills, so credit becomes a legacy advantage rather than a generational burden.

5 Actionable Steps to Build Financial Literacy

1. **Commit to Monthly Learning**
   o One book chapter, one podcast episode, or one course module per month.
2. **Follow Reliable Sources**
   o Use reputable financial education platforms and institutions.
3. **Apply What You Learn Immediately**
   o Small actions compound faster than passive reading.
4. **Teach It at Home**
   o Budgeting, saving, and credit basics make money an everyday conversation.
5. **Stay Aware of Scoring and Lending Shifts**
   o You don't need to be an expert, just informed enough to adapt.

Section 6: Plan for Major Life Events

Life events are where credit either supports you or stresses you. A relocation, a baby, a divorce, a career change, a medical event, a parent needing care, these moments create financial pressure. If you prepare for them, credit becomes a tool. If you don't, credit becomes a consequence.

Planning for life events is about timing. If you know you'll buy a home in 12 months, you should start protecting your utilization and avoiding unnecessary inquiries now. If you plan a career shift, you should build savings and reduce revolving debt before your income changes. If retirement is on the horizon, the goal is to reduce debt exposure and simplify your obligations. Credit strength isn't built in one week; it's built through habits aligned with your timeline.

Section 7: The Credit-Resilience Routine

Futureproofing is not a one-time cleanup. It is a routine you follow even when life is calm because calm is when you build the strength that protects you in the storm. I want readers to understand this: the best credit profiles are not built by "fixing problems." They are built by preventing problems through consistent, boring, disciplined actions.

A credit-resilience routine creates stability across the three things that matter most: **accuracy** (your reports are correct), **behavior** (your utilization and payments are stable), and **protection** (fraud and errors are caught early). When this routine becomes normal, your Middle Credit Score becomes less volatile. And when your score becomes less volatile, your life becomes more flexible.

5 Actionable Steps for The Monthly Credit-Resilience Routine

1. **Week 1: Review Balances and Utilization**
   - Keep utilization under 30%, aim for 10% when possible.
   - Identify one balance to reduce for trend stability.

2. **Week 2: Confirm Payments and Due Dates**
   - o Ensure autopay minimums are active.
   - o Schedule strategic paydowns before the statements cut.

3. **Week 3: Check Credit Monitoring Alerts**
   - o Review inquiries, new accounts, balance spikes, and bureau changes.
   - o Investigate anything you don't recognize immediately.

4. **Week 4: Strategy Reset**
   - o Ask: What's my next financial milestone?
   - o Align your credit behavior with your timeline (home, refinance, auto, business funding).

5. **Quarterly: Full Bureau Comparison**
   - o Identify inconsistencies between Experian, Equifax, and TransUnion.
   - o Dispute errors early before you need financing.

Section 8: The "Before You Apply" 60-Day Protection Plan

If there is one timeline that can change someone's financial life, it is the 60 days before a significant application. This is when lenders are most sensitive to risk signals, and it is when consumers accidentally make mistakes that cost them points and pricing. They open new accounts "to help their score," unaware that inquiries and new trade lines can hurt their scores. They carry higher balances because life is busy. They miss a due date by a few days. They ignore minor report errors until underwriting sees them. Then they're shocked when the Middle Credit Score doesn't reflect the effort they've been putting in.

This plan is designed to prevent those mistakes. It is about protecting your credit profile during the window when lenders scrutinize you most. Do this consistently, and you walk into underwriting positioned as low-risk, stable, accurate, and prepared.

6 Actionable Steps to a 60-Day Credit Protection Plan

1. **Freeze "New Credit"**
   - Avoid new credit cards, personal loans, furniture financing, and unnecessary inquiries.

2. **Stabilize Utilization**
   - Keep balances consistently low, not just "paid down once."
   - Consider mid-cycle payments if you tend to spike utilization.

3. **Audit All Three Bureaus**
   - Confirm accounts, balances, statuses, and personal data are accurate.
   - Address discrepancies immediately.

4. **Eliminate Payment Risk**
   - Autopay minimums and reminders for full payments.
   - No missed payments; none.

5. **Maintain Cash Buffer**
   o Keep emergency funds intact so you do not rely on revolving debt during the process.

6. **Document Anything Unusual**
   o If an account is disputed, resolved, or newly updated, keep paperwork organized.
   o Underwriting loves clarity.

Chapter 11 Closing: Building Credit That Survives Real Life

Futureproofing your credit is not about chasing a score. It is about building a structure that holds up under pressure. The people who win in the long term are not the ones who "fix credit"; they are the ones who build routines, buffers, and habits that keep their Middle Credit Score stable through job changes, medical surprises, economic shifts, and significant milestones.

This chapter gave you the blueprint for durability: a safety net to protect payment history, a diversified toolkit to prevent overreliance on revolving debt, awareness of market shifts, intentional use of technology, continued financial literacy, and planning for life events before they arrive. None of these moves is flashy, but they are powerful because they reduce volatility, which lenders punish.

When your credit profile stabilizes, your life becomes more flexible. You can move when opportunity calls. You can refinance when the timing is right. You can invest when the market shifts, and you can make decisions from confidence instead of urgency. That's what futureproofing is: building control before you need it.

The One Action Framework

The "Credit Futureproofing" Plan (30 / 60 / 90 Days)

Days 1–30: Build the Buffer + Audit Accuracy
Establish or reinforce your emergency fund and "bills first" budget. Pull and compare all three bureau reports, identify inconsistencies, and dispute clear errors with documentation. Set autopay minimums and calendar reminders to eliminate late-payment risk.

Days 31–60: Stabilize Trends + Reduce Fragility
Lower utilization deliberately aim under 30% and move toward 10% if possible. Pay down the highest-utilization accounts first and keep balances consistently low (not just once). Reduce financial pressure points by cutting or renegotiating one recurring expense and redirecting the savings into debt reduction or reserves.

Days 61–90: Lock in the Routine + Prepare for Major Moves
Commit to the credit-resilience routine: monthly utilization review, payment confirmation, monitoring alerts, and a quarterly bureau comparison. Avoid unnecessary new credit activity and maintain cash buffers. Align your credit behavior with your next milestone (home, refinance, auto, business funding) so your Middle Credit Score stays decision-ready.

Chapter 11 Final Takeaways

• Credit is a reputation built monthly, not a tool used occasionally
• Emergency reserves protect payment history and utilization during stress
• Diversification (income + financial buckets) reduces credit fragility
• Stable trends matter more now as scoring models evolve
• A consistent routine keeps your Middle Credit Score "decision-ready" year-round

Your Financial Journey

Turning Credit Strategy into a Repeatable Life Plan

If there is one truth I have learned after decades in real estate, lending, and credit coaching, it's this: financial success is rarely about one "magic" move. It is about alignment. When your credit, spending, and savings habits, and your long-term goals all point in the same direction, your results start to feel inevitable. That is what this chapter is designed to do: take everything you have learned about your Middle Credit Score®, credit strategy, budgeting, and long-term planning, and turn it into one cohesive plan that makes sense for your real life.

WHAT IS YOUR MIDDLE CREDIT SCORE?

A strong Middle Credit Score® is powerful, but it works best when a complete financial system supports it. I have seen consumers improve their score by 60, 80, even 100 points… and still feel anxious because they did not have savings, did not have a plan for emergencies, and did not know how to maintain the progress once the immediate goal was reached. That is why this chapter is not just about improving credit; it is about creating stability that lasts. Stability is what keeps you from slipping backward. Stability is what makes mortgage approval easier, makes interest rates more favorable, makes job transitions less terrifying, and makes financial opportunities feel accessible rather than intimidating.

Your financial journey is personal. Two people can have the same income and the same Middle Credit Score® and still end up in entirely different outcomes because one person has a plan and the other is reacting to life as it happens. The goal here is to move you into the driver's seat. When you know what matters most, when you can measure it, and when you can repeat the habits that create progress, you stop feeling "behind" and start feeling capable. And once you feel capable, you become consistent.

This chapter is your roadmap. You will define what you want, you will identify where you are, and you will build a system that keeps you moving forward month after month, year after year, because the real win is not a temporary score increase. The real win is building a financial life that can support your goals without constant stress.

Section 1: Define Your Financial Goals

Most people do not fail financially because they are lazy; they fail because they are unclear. When your goals are vague, your decisions become emotional. You spend when you are stressed, you avoid your numbers when you are overwhelmed, and you delay significant moves because you do not know what you are aiming for. Clear goals remove confusion. They give you a "why" strong enough to outlast the moments when motivation fades.

Defining financial goals is also how you stop treating money like an emergency and start treating it like a strategy. A goal is a decision with a direction. It tells you what to prioritize and what to postpone. It turns "I want to be better with money" into "I want to save $8,000 for a down payment in 12 months," or "I want to raise my Middle Credit Score to 740 so I can qualify for top-tier pricing," or "I want to eliminate credit card debt, so I stop paying interest every month."

Another reason goals matter is that your financial life has seasons. In one season, the priority might be stabilizing, catching up, protecting your credit, building a small savings cushion, and stopping the bleeding. In another season, it might be building, improving your Middle Credit Score®, expanding your income, or preparing for homeownership. In a later season, it might be multiplying investments, buying assets, and building generational wealth.

Goals help you identify which season you are in, so your actions match the reality of your life instead of someone else's. Do not overlook this: goals evolve. The goal you set today might shift as your income changes, as your family grows, or as your responsibilities increase. That does not mean you failed; it means you are living. The point is to revisit your goals consistently, refine them as needed, and keep moving forward with clarity.

5 Actionable Steps to Define Your Financial Goals

1. **Break Goals Into Categories**
   o Short-term (0–12 months): eliminate small debts, bring utilization down, build starter savings
   o Mid-term (1–5 years): down payment, home purchase prep, business startup, debt payoff
   o Long-term (5+ years): retirement, investing, generational wealth, paid-off home

2. **Use the SMART Framework**
   o Specific, Measurable, Achievable, Relevant, Time-bound

3. **Put Deadlines on Every Goal**
   o Deadlines create urgency and prevent "someday" from becoming "never"

4. **Track Progress Weekly**
   o Progress isn't luck, it's measurement and repetition

5. **Reassess Quarterly**
   o Adjust goals when income, expenses, or life priorities change

From My Client File - Example 85 (Chapter 12):
Turning Dreams into Actionable Goals

I worked with a couple, Karen and Leroy, who had big dreams but no structure. They wanted a home, a business, and college savings for their kids, but they were also carrying credit card debt and felt like they were running in place. They were not lacking ambition. They were lacking sequence. Everything felt urgent, so nothing moved.

We started by turning their dreams into categories and timelines. First came stability: eliminate high-interest debt and build an emergency fund so unexpected expenses would not derail them. Then came credit strength: reduce utilization, tighten up payment habits, and improve their Middle Credit Score so homeownership could happen on favorable terms. Only after those two were in motion did we map out the longer-term pieces: business savings, college planning, and retirement contributions.

Once their goals were clear, their decision-making changed. They stopped guessing. They stopped spending emotionally. They started tracking, and their confidence grew because the plan made progress visible. Their success was not just getting the house; it was learning how to build a roadmap that made future wins repeatable.

Section 2: Assess Your Current Financial Situation

Before you build a plan, you must tell the truth about your starting point. Not an emotional truth. A factual truth. Because if your numbers are unclear, your strategy becomes shaky. The best financial plans are not built on hope; they are built on awareness. Awareness gives you leverage. It shows you what is working, what is draining you, and what is quietly holding you back.

This is where your Middle Credit Score matters most. Your Middle Credit Score is not just a number; it is a gatekeeper. It influences approvals, interest rates, insurance pricing, and sometimes even employment screening. But your score does not exist in isolation. It is connected to your payment history, utilization, report accuracy, and the consistency of your financial habits. Assessing your situation means examining the whole picture: your credit, cash flow, debts, assets, and monthly obligations.

It also means identifying hidden problems. Many consumers do not realize their budget is leaking money through small habits. Others do not learn that a single reporting error is costing them better pricing. Some people assume they "do not make enough," when the real issue is that their debt payments are consuming their flexibility. This section is about finding those leverage points because one adjustment in the right area can create momentum across everything else.

Finally, your financial assessment is not about judgment. It is about control. When you know your numbers, you make better decisions. When you do not, you react. And reaction is expensive.

5 Actionable Steps to Assess Your Current Financial Situation

1. **Audit Your Credit Profile**
   - o Pull bureau reports and confirm accounts, balances, statuses, and late payments

2. **Calculate Your Real Monthly Cash Flow**
   - o Income minus fixed bills minus variable spending

3. **List Assets and Liabilities**
   - o Everything you own vs. everything you owe

4. **Calculate Your Debt-to-Income Ratio**
   - o Total monthly debt payments ÷ gross monthly income

5. **Identify the "Big 3 Leaks"**
   - High-interest debt, high utilization, and inconsistent spending

From My Client File - Example 86 (Chapter 12): The Power of Getting Honest with the Numbers

---

Steven was self-employed and earning a solid income, but his financial life felt unstable because it was not clearly defined. He did not know his actual monthly spending, had not mapped his debt payoff, and assumed his Middle Credit Score was "good enough" because nothing had gone wrong yet. When he started exploring homeownership, that lack of clarity turned into stress; the system was not rejecting him; it was exposing him.

When we pulled his reports, the issues became clear. An outdated item and a single reporting error were quietly suppressing his Middle Credit Score, while untracked spending kept utilization higher than he realized. Instead of guessing, we built a real budget, one rooted in actual numbers, not ideal behavior. Once Steven saw exactly where his money was going, the emotional fog lifted. Awareness changed behavior faster than motivation ever could.

Within six months, he reduced utilization, corrected the reporting issue, and strengthened his Middle Credit Score enough to re-enter the conversation with confidence. But the most critical shift was not the approval, it was ownership. Steven learned that honesty with the numbers creates leverage. When you stop avoiding the truth, the truth becomes a plan.

Section 3: Create a Budget Aligned with Your Goals

A budget is not a punishment; it is a strategy. When your budget aligns with your goals, it becomes a tool that buys you freedom. It tells your money where to go before life tells it where it went. It creates structure, and structure creates peace. Most financial anxiety does not come from not having enough money; it comes from not knowing where it is going.

Your budget should reflect your priorities, not your impulses. If your goal is to strengthen your Middle Credit Score, then your budget should support consistent on-time payments, shrink utilization, and reduce high-interest debt. If your goal is homeownership, your budget should support savings for a down payment, closing costs, and reserves. If your goal is long-term stability, your budget should build savings and reduce dependency on revolving debt.

The secret to budgeting is sustainability. Most people create budgets that are too strict, and then they abandon them. A substantial budget is realistic. It includes space for the food you eat, the expenses you incur, and the small joys that keep you consistent. The goal is not perfection. The goal is repetition.

And this is where automation matters. When savings and debt payments happen automatically, your plan stays intact even when motivation fades or life gets noisy. Automation removes emotion from execution and replaces it with consistency. That consistency is what builds momentum; and momentum is what turns a budget from an intention into a system you can live with.

5 Actionable Steps to Build a Goal-Aligned Budget

1. **Separate Fixed vs. Variable Costs**
2. **Assign Every Dollar a Job**
3. **Automate Savings and Debt Payments**

4. **Track Weekly, Adjust Monthly**
5. **Build a "Reality Buffer"**
   - A small category for unexpected expenses, so the plan stays intact

From My Client Files - Example 87 (Chapter 12): The Budget That Built a Home

---

Lisa and Michael did not have an income problem; they had a visibility problem. Money was coming in consistently, but it was leaking out in ways they could not clearly track. Savings felt optional, progress felt slow, and homeownership remained a vague goal instead of a defined plan. Once we laid everything out, it became apparent: without structure, even good income can feel unstable.

We rebuilt their approach around alignment, not restriction. Their budget was redesigned to align with their actual goal of buying a home, not just covering monthly expenses. They trimmed unnecessary variable spending, automated savings, so progress did not depend on motivation, and assigned every dollar a purpose. The system was not extreme, but it was intentional and, most importantly, sustainable.

Over time, the budget did more than grow a down payment. It reshaped how they saw themselves. They stopped feeling like people who wanted to be homeowners and started behaving like people who were preparing to be homeowners. Their Middle Credit Score strengthened as utilization stabilized, savings became predictable, and financial decisions became calmer and more deliberate. That is what aligned budgeting does; it does not just change numbers. It changes identity, and identity is what turns plans into outcomes.

Section 4: Strengthen Your Middle Credit Score

Your Middle Credit Score is one of the most potent financial levers you have. It influences the cost of borrowing, the quality of loan terms, and the ease of approvals. When your Middle Credit Score improves, your money goes further because you pay less for the same opportunity. That is why strengthening it is not just a "credit goal." It is a long-term wealth strategy.

Improving your Middle Credit Score requires understanding what moves the needle. It is rarely complicated, but it does require discipline. Payment history is foundational. Utilization is a significant lever, and the accuracy of reporting matters more than most people realize. The timing of your payments, how much you carry, and how consistently you reduce balances can make the difference between slow improvement and real momentum.

A strong Middle Credit Score also protects you. Life happens, and when it does, strong credit keeps options open. It gives you flexibility in emergencies. It makes refinancing possible. It keeps your financial life from becoming expensive during tough seasons. Credit strength is not about impressing lenders; it is about maintaining flexibility when life applies pressure.

The key is consistency. Small actions, repeated monthly, create significant results over time.

Section 5: Build an Emergency Fund

An emergency fund is the quiet hero of financial stability. It prevents minor problems from turning into financial disasters.

Without it, life's surprises get financed. And when emergencies are financed with high-interest credit, your Middle Credit Score takes a hit from utilization spikes, missed payments, and rising debt stress.

Building an emergency fund is not about waiting until you have "extra money." It is about creating the habit of saving even when the amount feels small. A $25 contribution is not about the dollar amount; it is about the identity you are building: "I prepare." Consistency matters more than intensity, especially in the beginning.

An emergency fund also protects your mindset. When you know you have reserves, you make better decisions. You are less likely to panic. You are less likely to accept bad loan terms. You are less likely to rely on debt out of fear. That peace of mind is worth building.

Section 6: Invest in Your Financial Education

Your income matters, but your understanding matters too. Financial education is what turns money into strategy instead of stress. It is what helps you recognize opportunity, avoid traps, and build a long-term plan that does not collapse every time life changes.

The financial world evolves, with credit scoring changes, shifting lending rules, changing interest rate environments, and new tools entering the market. When you stay educated, you stay powerful. Education keeps you from being surprised. It helps you ask better questions and make more brilliant moves.

Education is not only for you. When you understand money, you create a ripple effect. You help your family. You teach your kids. You become the person in your circle who can explain what most people avoid. That's how financial literacy becomes legacy.

Section 7: Monitor Progress and Adjust

A financial plan is not a one-time document; it is a living system. If you do not review it, you drift. And drift is expensive. Monitoring progress creates accountability. It tells you what is improving, what is stuck, and what needs adjustment before it becomes a problem.

Quarterly check-ins are where long-term success is built. Not because life is perfect, but because you catch issues early. Your Middle Credit Score may dip, your spending may creep up, your savings may stall, and your debt payoff may slow. Reviews protect your progress and keep your plan honest.

This section is also where motivation becomes sustainable. When you track progress, you see wins. And when you see wins, you keep going. Momentum is built by proof. Proof comes from measurement.

Section 8: Build Your "One-Page Financial Command Center"

A strong plan must be simple enough to use. That is why I recommend creating a one-page "Financial Command Center," a single snapshot that shows the numbers that matter most. When your financial world is scattered across apps, statements, and mental notes, it becomes easier to avoid. When it's organized, it becomes easier to lead.

This one-page snapshot becomes your weekly and monthly guide. It keeps you focused on what moves the needle: your Middle Credit Score, your savings, your debt payoff, your budget categories, and your key deadlines. It also reduces stress because you stop guessing and start knowing.

A command center isn't about complexity. It is about clarity. And clarity creates consistent action.

Section 9: Understanding the importance of a Financial Plan

From My Client Files - Example 88 (Chapter 12): Helen's Road to Financial Stability

---

Helen was a dedicated teacher who wanted homeownership but felt boxed in by student loans and inconsistent savings. On paper, she was doing "okay," but emotionally, she felt stuck, as if progress was always just out of reach. The issue was not income or effort. It was a lack of structure. Her goals were not clearly defined, and her budget was leaking in small, untracked ways, quietly limiting her options.

Once we slowed everything down and looked at the whole picture, the path forward became clear. Helen defined a realistic goal, not an aggressive, burnout-inducing plan, but one that fit her life. We identified and corrected credit report errors, automated her savings so consistency didn't depend on willpower, and focused on reducing utilization in a controlled, repeatable way. Nothing about the plan was extreme. It was intentional.

Within months, the results showed up not just in her numbers, but in her mindset. Her Middle Credit Score® improved, her emergency fund began to grow, and, for the first time, the future felt manageable rather than intimidating. The most important shift was not financial, it was internal. The plan gave her control, and control gave her confidence, and once confidence shows up, consistency follows.

From My Client Files - Example 89 (Chapter 12): Samuel's Journey to Homeownership

Samuel was a single father with no shortage of motivation, but a minimal margin for error. Every dollar had an assignment, and every unexpected expense put pressure on it. He wanted homeownership, but more than that, he wanted stability for his child. What held him back wasn't discipline or desire; it was the absence of a clear, prioritized plan that matched his reality.

We stripped the process down to essentials. Samuel's plan focused on three non-negotiables: reducing high-interest debt, building starter reserves, and stabilizing monthly cash flow. There were no shortcuts and no unrealistic timelines. Each month, he deliberately targeted utilization, protected his payment history, and tracked progress with intention. Nothing was left to guesswork, because guesswork is expensive when your margin is tight.

Over time, consistency did what intensity never could. His Middle Credit Score® rose steadily, his debt-to-income ratio improved, and his financial profile began telling a story lenders trust. When the time came to explore mortgage options, Samuel was not just prepared. The access he gained was not accidental. It was earned through structure, repetition, and a plan that respected both his goals and his responsibilities.

From My Client Files - Example 90 (Chapter 12): Nicole's Plan for Financial Freedom

---

Nicole wasn't struggling because of her income; she was working because her income lacked structure. On paper, she was doing well. In reality, her spending was reactive, her savings were inconsistent, and her financial progress depended too much on willpower. She felt stuck, not because she lacked opportunity, but because there was no system guiding her decisions month to month.

The turning point came when we aligned her budget with her actual goals instead of her habits. We automated savings, assigned every dollar a role, and focused intentionally on utilization reduction. As balances dropped, her Middle Credit Score improved not through drastic cuts, but through consistent behavior. The automation removed emotion from the process, which allowed progress to continue even during busy or stressful periods.

What changed most wasn't just her numbers; it was her mindset. Nicole learned that financial freedom is not created by earning more alone; it is produced by managing better. Once her structure was in place, she could enjoy her lifestyle without sacrificing long-term growth. Short-term choices stopped competing with future goals because the system supported both. That's what real financial balance looks like.

Chapter 12 Closing: From Strategy to a Financial Identity

This chapter was not about doing more; it was about doing things in the correct order, with intention. Financial progress becomes sustainable when your goals, habits, and systems are aligned. When alignment exists, you stop relying on motivation and start relying on structure. That is when results stop feeling fragile and start feeling repeatable.

What you have built through this chapter is not a checklist; it is a framework. A way to define where you are going, measure where you are, and make decisions that move you forward without constant stress. A strong Middle Credit Score plays a central role in that framework, but it only works when supported by budgeting discipline, emergency reserves, education, and consistent review. This is how progress becomes permanent instead of temporary.

When your financial life is structured, confidence replaces anxiety. You stop reacting to bills, credit reports, and life events as emergencies. You begin making decisions from clarity. That shift from responding to leading is what separates people who "try to get ahead" from people who do. This chapter marks that shift.

The One Action Framework

The "Aligned Financial System" Plan (30 / 60 / 90 Days)

Days 1–30: Clarify Direction + Establish Visibility
Define your financial goals across short-, mid-, and long-term

timelines. Pull and review all three credit reports, calculate actual cash flow, list assets and liabilities, and build your one-page Financial Command Center. Automate minimum payments and savings so your plan continues to function even when life gets busy.

Days 31–60: Stabilize Behavior + Reduce Friction
Align your budget with your top goals and eliminate the most significant financial leaks: high-interest debt, rising utilization, and inconsistent spending. Reduce credit card balances deliberately, protect payment history, and build or reinforce your emergency fund so surprises do not derail progress.

Days 61–90: Lock the System + Reinforce Consistency
Commit to quarterly reviews, monthly credit monitoring, and weekly budget check-ins. Adjust goals as needed without abandoning structure. Keep utilization trending down, savings trending up, and habits aligned with your next milestone: homeownership, refinancing, career moves, or long-term wealth building.

Chapter 12 Final Takeaways

• Alignment turns effort into momentum
• A strong Middle Credit Score works best inside a complete system
• Visibility creates control; control creates confidence
• Budgets succeed when they're realistic and automated
• Emergency funds protect both credit and decision-making
• Consistent review prevents drift and protects progress

From Understanding to Ownership

How Credit Knowledge Becomes a Lifelong Advantage

If you are reading this final chapter, you have already done something that most people never do; you did not just look for motivation, you looked for understanding. You chose to learn the "why" behind your credit, the truth behind your Middle Credit Score®, and the real habits that create long-term financial stability. That decision matters more than you realize, because once you understand the system, you stop feeling powerless inside it.

FROM UNDERSTANDING TO OWNERSHIP

I want to say this clearly: you did not get here by luck. You got here because you were willing to face your numbers, challenge old habits, and replace confusion with clarity. That is not easy. Most people avoid credit until they need it, and by then, the cost is higher, and the options are fewer. But you chose a different route; you chose preparation, and preparation changes everything.

This book was never meant to be "information." It was meant to be a transformation. That is why we focused on the Middle Credit Score®: it is the score that often determines approvals, pricing, and opportunities. It is the score that can decide whether or not you qualify for the best rates or pay thousands more over the life of a loan. But even more than that, understanding your Middle Credit Score is how you stop treating credit like a mystery and start using it like a tool.

Now you are in the best part of the journey, the part where your progress becomes permanent. The real win is not a temporary improvement; it is building a lifestyle and a mindset that keep you moving forward. The kind of mindset that keeps you steady during setbacks, disciplined during distractions, and confident during major life decisions.

As you close this book, understand this: this is not the end. This is you becoming the person who handles money differently. This is you moving forward with your eyes open, your plan intact, and your confidence earned.

Section 1: Track Your Progress Like It Matters, Because It Does

A financial plan doesn't protect you unless you revisit it, and your Middle Credit Score® does not stay strong because you improved it once; it stays strong because you maintain the habits that built it. That is why tracking is not optional. It is the difference between momentum and drift.

Think about how life works: bills change, income changes, family needs change, emergencies happen, and priorities shift. If you do not review your budget and credit habits regularly, you will wake up one day wondering how things got off track. Not because you failed, but because you stopped measuring, and anything you do not measure eventually starts making decisions for you.

Tracking your progress is also how you stay encouraged. When people give up on financial goals, it is usually because they don't feel progress, even when progress is happening. But when you track your Middle Credit Score, your debt reduction, your savings growth, and your spending patterns, you create proof, and proof fuels consistency.

Let me add something I have seen repeatedly: tracking removes guesswork. The moment you stop guessing and start knowing, you move from reaction to leadership.

6 Actionable Steps to Track Progress and Adjust

1. **Break Goals into Milestones**
   Turn big goals into small wins you can measure monthly.

2. **Set Quarterly Review Dates**
    Choose a recurring date every three months, on the same day, every quarter.

3. **Measure Your Middle Credit Score Trends**
    Don't obsess over daily changes; watch the direction over time.

4. **Adjust for Life Events Quickly**
    New job, new baby, relocation, medical bills, update the plan immediately.

5. **Celebrate Progress on Purpose**
    Wins reinforce habits. Reward yourself within your budget.

6. **Use a Journal to Document Growth**
    A Middle Credit Score Journal makes progress visible, and visibility builds belief.

Section 2: Protect Your Momentum When Life Gets Loud

The reason most people fall backward is not that they do not know what to do. It is because life gets loud. Stress shows up. A surprise expense hits alongside a job change. The holidays come. Motivation dips, and in noisy moments, people revert to what is familiar; even when what is familiar is not healthy.

That is why sustaining momentum is about building systems, not relying on mood. Systems protect you during the seasons when you are tired, distracted, or overwhelmed. A system can be as simple as automated savings, automatic payments, a weekly budget check-in, and a monthly credit review. Those small routines keep you steady.

Momentum is also emotional. You must stay connected to your "why." The strongest financial plans are not driven by fear; they are driven by purpose. Homeownership. Stability. Freedom. Family. Peace of mind. When your "why" is strong, your habits become easier to maintain.

Remember this: you do not need perfect months. You need consistent months. You do not need flawless discipline. You need repeatable habits.

5 Actionable Steps to Sustain Momentum

1. **Create Monthly Credit Routines**
   A 10-minute monthly review beats a crisis-driven overhaul.
2. **Automate the Essentials**
   Automate payments and savings so progress continues without willpower.
3. **Build a "Real Life" Category in Your Budget**
   A buffer category keeps one surprise from breaking your plan.
4. **Keep Utilization Low Even When Money Is Tight**
   Reduce balances gradually but protect the ratio.
5. **Stay Connected to the Goal**
   Read your goals weekly. Keep them visible.

Section 3: Use Your Middle Credit Score as Leverage; Not Just a Number

Your Middle Credit Score® is not a trophy. It is leverage. It gives you negotiating power. It is the difference between paying more and keeping more. And when you understand that you stop chasing approval, you start choosing opportunity.

When your Middle Credit Score is strong, lenders compete for you. Insurance pricing often improves. Access to credit becomes cheaper. Refinancing becomes possible. Opportunities become realistic. That is why the goal isn't just to "raise your score." The goal is to put yourself in a position where your financial options expand.

But leverage only matters if you use it wisely. Strong credit is not an excuse to take on more debt; it's a tool to lower your cost of living and grow your long-term stability. If you qualify for better terms, use them to strengthen your foundation: lower interest rates, lower payments, more savings, more investing, more breathing room.

You are thinking bigger: homeownership, investment property, business funding. Your Middle Credit Score can be one of the tools that helps you move faster and safer.

5 Actionable Steps to Maximize Your Middle Credit Score

1. **Negotiate Interest Rates and Terms**
   Ask for better pricing, strong credit earns it.
2. **Use Pre-Qualification First**
   Limit hard inquiries by exploring options the smart way.

3. **Plan Big Purchases 6–12 Months Ahead**
   Timing matters. Preparation lowers costs.

4. **Use Credit to Build Assets**
   Focus on assets, not lifestyle upgrades.

5. **Set a New 6-Month Target**
   One measurable goal that forces forward motion.

Section 4: Keep Growing; Financial Literacy Is a Lifestyle

Financial literacy is not a chapter you finish. It is a lifestyle you live. The moment you assume you "already know," life has a way of humbling you. Markets change. Rates change. Credit models evolve. New tools show up. New risks show up. Staying educated keeps you protected and keeps you ahead.

The most financially stable people are not always the highest earners. Often, they are the most consistent learners. They stay aware. They ask questions. They make decisions from clarity, not pressure, and they do not rely on luck; they rely on habits.

This is also where legacy begins, because once you understand money and credit, you can teach it. You can help your children start smarter. You can help your family avoid mistakes. You can become the person in your circle who breaks generational patterns.

5 Actionable Steps to Stay Committed to Growth

1. **Schedule Quarterly Financial Check-Ins**
2. **Commit to One New Lesson Per Month**
3. **Talk to a Trusted Professional When Needed**
4. **Teach One Person What You have Learned**
5. **Keep Your Plan Flexible, Not Fragile**

From My Client Files - Example 91 (Chapter 13): The Difference Between Temporary Improvement and Permanent Change

I have worked with people who raised their Middle Credit Score quickly but did not change their habits. And within a year, they were right back where they started. I have also worked with people who improved more slowly but built routines that lasted. Those are the people who ended up buying homes, refinancing into better terms, and building absolute financial stability.

One client in particular stands out. She did not have a perfect income, but she committed. She tracked her spending weekly. She kept her utilization under control. She built a small emergency fund first, then grew it over time. Her Middle Credit Score improved steadily, not dramatically, and that steady improvement changed her life, not because of one big move, but because she became consistent.

That's the outcome I want for you: not a moment of success, but a lifetime of control.

From My Client Files - Example 92 (Chapter 13): Rebuilding Trust After Financial Avoidance

Marcus was intelligent, capable, and employed, but completely disconnected from his finances. Not because he did not care, but because he had learned to associate money with stress and shame. He avoided his credit reports, ignored balances unless something broke, and told himself he would "deal with it later." Later turned into years.

When Marcus finally sat down with his numbers, his Middle Credit Score was in the low 600s, not disastrous, but fragile. Late payments were not frequent, but they were inconsistent. Utilization crept up slowly over time. Nothing was catastrophic, yet everything was quietly expensive.

The breakthrough was not tactical; it was emotional. We reframed the process from "fixing mistakes" to "earning trust back." Trust in the system. Trust in himself. He committed to simple routines: monthly reviews, automated payments, and utilization checkpoints. No shortcuts. No panic moves.

Within a year, his Middle Credit Score stabilized in the mid-700s. More importantly, Marcus stopped avoiding his finances. He became proactive. The anxiety disappeared because clarity replaced it. His success came not from intensity but from consistency.

Lesson: *Credit stability begins the moment avoidance ends.*

From My Client Files - Example 93 (Chapter 13): When Income Is not the Problem—Structure Is

Angela earned six figures and still felt broke. On paper, she was "doing everything right."
In reality, her finances were unstructured. Spending was reactive. Savings were inconsistent. Credit was used for convenience instead of strategy.

Her Middle Credit Score hovered around 680, not terrible, but not reflective of her earning power. High utilization on a few cards was the main culprit. She assumed the solution was to make more money. It was not.

We rebuilt her system from the inside out. Fixed categories. Automated savings. Intentional debt paydown focused on utilization ratios, not balances alone. Her awareness changed her behavior.

Six months later, her Middle Credit Score crossed 740. Her savings account grew for the first time without effort. She did not change careers. She changed the structure.

Lesson: *High income does not create stability; systems do.*

From My Client Files - Example 94 (Chapter 13):
Protecting Progress Through a Life Transition

After a divorce, Kevin's finances were shaken not because of recklessness, but because everything changed at once. New housing. New expenses. New emotional stress. His Middle Credit Score dipped quickly as balances rose and routines broke.

Kevin assumed recovery would take years. It did not, but only because we focused on protecting what still worked instead of starting over.

We rebuilt payment automation first. Then, it addressed utilization incrementally. No significant credit activity. No emotional spending. Just stability.

Within nine months, his Middle Credit Score returned to pre-divorce levels. But the real win was that he learned how to protect his credit during chaos, a skill that lasts longer than any score.

Lesson: *Credit resilience matters most when life is not calm.*

From My Client Files - Example 95 (Chapter 13):
Turning Credit Knowledge into Generational Impact

Denise did not come to me for herself; she came for her kids. She had rebuilt her credit years earlier, but realized she had no plan to pass that knowledge forward. Her fear was not debt, it was repetition.

We did not focus on optimization. We focused on education. She learned how to explain utilization, payment history, and credit traps in plain language. She helped her oldest child open a credit responsibly. She monitored, not controlled.

Years later, her children entered adulthood with strong credit, no panic, and clear habits. Denise did not just improve a score; she interrupted a cycle.

Lesson: *Financial literacy becomes a legacy when it is shared.*

From My Client Files - Example 96 (Chapter 13): When "Good Enough" Was Costing Thousands

Tom believed his credit was okay. His Middle Credit Score hovered around 690, and approvals were rarely an issue. He could get loans. He could get insurance. He could move forward. What he did not realize was that "approved" does not mean "optimized." Every approval came with slightly higher interest rates, higher insurance premiums, and less favorable terms, and over time, those slight differences quietly drained his finances. He accepted it as normal because he did not know there was another level.

Once Tom understood how pricing tiers worked, everything changed. We didn't chase a dramatic score jump; we focused on precision. We targeted utilization below 10%, corrected minor reporting inconsistencies, and improved the timing of payments so his profile reflected stability rather than just adequacy. These were not radical changes. They were intentional ones. And they moved him into a better pricing tier without adding risk or complexity.

*The outcome was not just a higher score; it was lower monthly costs across the board. Over time, those savings compounded into real money that stayed in Tom's pocket instead of going to interest and fees. The lesson here is critical: **approval is the floor, not the goal**. Optimized credit changes what you pay for life, and when you understand that difference, you stop settling for "good enough" and start building long-term advantage.*

From My Client Files - Example 97 (Chapter 13): The Moment Credit Became a Tool, not a Fear

---

Samantha did not avoid credit because she was careless; she avoided it because she was afraid. Early mistakes had convinced her that avoiding credit altogether was the safest option. She paid cash, avoided applications, and told herself she was being responsible. But over time, that avoidance quietly cost her flexibility, opportunity, and confidence. When life required options, she did not have them, not because she lacked discipline, but because she lacked a usable credit profile.

We approached her situation intentionally and without judgment. One account. One habit. One routine at a time. The goal was not to rush results; it was to rebuild trust between Samantha and the credit system as she learned how utilization, payment timing, and reporting worked, and credit stopped feeling emotional and started feeling mechanical. What once felt risky became predictable. What once felt overwhelming became manageable.

Her Middle Credit Score rose steadily, but the real change was internal. Samantha stopped fearing financial decisions because she finally understood them. She learned when to say yes, when to say no, and most importantly, why. Credit was no longer something that happened to her. It became a tool she could use deliberately, and that shift from fear to fluency is what lasting financial confidence looks like.

Chapter 13 Closing: The Moment You Become the Person Who Builds Wealth on Purpose

If you have made it to this final chapter, you have done more than learn about credit; you have changed your relationship with it. You now understand what most consumers never take the time to understand: your Middle Credit Score is not random, and your financial future is not luck. It is the outcome of habits, systems, and decisions repeated over time.

This book gave you the foundation: how credit works, how Tri-Merge reporting impacts real approvals, why lenders rely on the middle credit score, how to build credit without falling into debt traps, how to protect your profile through life events, and how to future-proof your progress with structure. The real win is not what you read; it's what you keep doing. Confidence does not come from knowing the system once, it comes from living in a way that keeps the system working for you.

When your credit habits are consistent, your life becomes flexible. You do not have to panic when an opportunity appears. You do not have to fear a big purchase, a move, a new season of life, or a financial curveball. You become the person who can respond with clarity because your plan is already in place. That is the moment everything changes: you stop hoping for financial stability and start operating from it.

The One Action Framework

The "Finish Strong" Plan (30 / 60 / 90 Days)

Days 1–30: Lock the Routine + Track What Matters
Start (or continue) your Middle Credit Score Journal and build your weekly habit of measurement: utilization, spending awareness, savings progress, and due dates. Set all minimum payments to autopay, add reminders for full-payoff or strategic paydowns, and schedule your following quarterly credit review on the calendar now before life gets loud.

Days 31–60: Protect Momentum + Create Real-Life Buffers
Add a "real life" category to your budget and begin building or
reinforcing emergency reserves. Small deposits count. Keep
utilization trending down consistently (not just once). Reduce one
recurring expense and redirect that money into reserves or debt
reduction. Stability is created by removing pressure points before
they become crises.

Days 61–90: Use Leverage + Set the Next Milestone
Set a specific next target: a Middle Credit Score range, a debt
payoff milestone, an emergency fund number, or a
homeownership timeline. Prepare for major moves 6–12 months
in advance by freezing unnecessary new credit, keeping balances
low, and maintaining clean reporting. Strong credit is leverage; use
it to reduce your cost of living and build assets, not to take on
lifestyle debt.

Chapter 13 Final Takeaways

• The Middle Credit Score is leverage, use it to lower costs and
expand options
• Systems, not motivation, protect momentum
• Tracking turns anxiety into clarity, and clarity into action
• Consistency beats perfection. Repeatable habits create
permanent change
• Your plan must stay alive: review it, adjust it, and protect it
through every season

You are not the same person you were when you started this
book. You are more aware. More prepared. More strategic, and

that's the real victory. Your financial future is no longer something that happens to you; it is something you build.

Your Credit Is No Longer a Mystery, It's a Tool!

Credit Terms Explained — Plain English, Real Impact

Section 1: Core Credit Concepts

Credit Behavior

Credit behavior is how your day-to-day actions, such as balances carried, payment timing, usage patterns, and account management signals either stability or stress over time. Lenders don't just care that you pay; they care **how** you use credit between payments.

Consistently high balances, even when paid on time, can signal dependency. Strategic usage, timely payments, and controlled balances signal discipline. Over time, behavior becomes reputation.
The mistake most people make is treating the score as the objective.

The score is the **output**, not the input. It reacts to habits. When balances stay controlled, payments remain consistent, and activity is stable, the score improves naturally. When behavior becomes reactive or erratic, the score reflects that just as quickly.

Core Credit Concepts: Referenced in Chapter(s)
Credit Behavior → Chapters 2, 3, 6, 13
Core Credit Concepts: Representative Client File Example(s)
Credit Behavior → Ch. 6, 13 → Examples 50, 91, 97

Credit Identity

Credit identity is the long-term reputation you build through repeated habits. It's not defined by one score, one mistake, or one win: it's the pattern that forms over time.

When your credit identity is strong, lenders see continuity, responsibility, and predictability. That identity often matters more than any single snapshot, because it tells lenders who you are *as a borrower*, not just where you landed this month.

Core Credit Concepts: Referenced in Chapter(s)
Credit Identity → Chapters 3, 7, 13
Core Credit Concepts: Representative Client File Example(s)
Credit Identity → Ch. 3, 13 → Examples 92, 95

Credit Literacy

Credit literacy is the ability to understand, interpret, and strategically manage credit, not just monitor a score. It's knowing **what moves the needle**, when timing matters, and how lenders actually evaluate risk.
Financially literate borrowers don't panic over fluctuations. They recognize cause and effect, plan ahead of decisions, and use credit intentionally rather than emotionally.

Core Credit Concepts: Referenced in Chapter(s)
Credit Literacy → Chapters 1, 4, 7, 13
Core Credit Concepts: Representative Client File Example(s)
Credit Literacy → Ch. 7, 13 → Examples 91, 97

Credit Profile

Your credit profile is the complete story behind the score. It includes open and closed accounts, balances, payment history, account age, inquiries, and critically, how consistently this information is reported across bureaus.

Lenders don't just glance at a number. They scan the profile for **patterns of stability or risk**. Two people can share the same score and receive very different outcomes because one profile looks steady and intentional, while the other looks fragile or inconsistent. The profile is where lending decisions are truly made.

Core Credit Concepts: Referenced in Chapter(s)
Credit Profile → Chapters 4, 5, 10
Core Credit Concepts: Representative Client File Example(s)
Credit Profile → Ch. 5, 10 → Examples 33, 37, 96

Credit Score

A credit score is a numerical summary of how lenders interpret your past credit behavior. It is not a judgment of character, effort, or intelligence; it is a **risk indicator**, built from observable patterns: how consistently you pay, how much of your available credit you use, how long you've managed accounts, and how stable your behavior has been over time.

Core Credit Concepts: Referenced in Chapter(s)
Credit Score → Chapters 1, 2, 4
Core Credit Concepts: Representative Client File Example(s)
Credit Score → Ch. 4, 6 → Examples 33, 50

Credit Stability

Credit stability is the consistency of your credit habits across months and years. It reflects whether your profile appears calm and predictable or reactive and fragile.

Lenders trust stability more than short-term improvement. A borrower whose profile improves slowly but steadily is often viewed as lower risk than someone who spikes scores quickly through temporary actions.

Core Credit Concepts: Referenced in Chapter(s)
Credit Stability → Chapters 6, 10, 13
Core Credit Concepts: Representative Client File Example(s)
Credit Stability → Ch. 6, 13 → Examples 91, 94

Credit Volatility

Credit volatility refers to frequent or abrupt changes in balances, inquiries, accounts, or payment behavior that make a file appear unstable, even when scores are technically acceptable. Volatility introduces uncertainty. It suggests that a borrower's situation may be changing faster than the data can explain. Lenders price uncertainty conservatively, which means volatility often costs money even when approvals are granted.

Core Credit Concepts: Referenced in Chapter(s)
Credit Volatility → Chapters 6, 10
Core Credit Concepts: Representative Client File Example(s)
Credit Volatility → Ch. 6 → Examples 50, 96

Creditworthiness

Creditworthiness is how reliable you appear to a lender based on **behavior over time**, not income alone, and not perfection. It answers the unspoken question: *Can this borrower be trusted to manage obligations predictably?*

Strong creditworthiness is built through consistency, on-time payments, controlled utilization, accurate reporting, and patience. When lenders perceive low risk, they compete for you with better pricing. When they perceive uncertainty, they protect themselves by charging more.

Core Credit Concepts: Referenced in Chapter(s)
Creditworthiness → Chapters 7, 10
Core Credit Concepts: Representative Client File Example(s)
Creditworthiness → Ch. 7, 10 → Examples 94, 96

Middle Credit Score®

When a lender pulls credit, they typically receive three scores: one from each bureau. In many lending decisions, especially mortgages, lenders use the **middle score**, not the highest, or the lowest. That single number often controls both **approval and pricing**.

Understanding this changes how you approach credit. You stop chasing the best-looking number and start strengthening the score that determines cost. This is where many borrowers lose money, not because their credit is bad, but because they don't know which score the system will use against them

Core Credit Concepts: Referenced in Chapter(s)
Middle Credit Score® → *Chapters 1, 4, 5, 10, 13*
Core Credit Concepts: Representative Client File Example(s)
Middle Credit Score® → *Ch. 5, 10, 13* → *Examples 33, 37, 96*

The **Middle Credit Score** (often called the **median credit score**) is the score lenders commonly use—especially in **U.S. mortgage lending**—when they pull your credit from multiple bureaus.

What it means

When a lender checks your credit, they usually get scores from the **three major credit bureaus**:
- Experian
- Equifax
- TransUnion

The **middle credit score** is:
- **The score in the middle** when all three are listed from lowest to highest.

Example
If your scores are:
- Experian: **680**
- Equifax: **720**
- TransUnion: **700**

Ordered: 680, **700**, 720 → **Middle credit score = 700**
Special cases

- **If only two scores are available**: lenders usually take the **lower** of the two.

- **If only one score is available**: that score is used.

Why it matters

- Mortgage programs (FHA, VA, Conventional) base **approval, interest rate, and terms** on the middle score—not an average.

- When applying jointly, lenders typically use the **lower middle score** between borrowers.

Credit scores generally fall within broad ranges that lenders use to assess relative risk, not as absolute pass-or-fail lines. These ranges are not guarantees, and they are not universal; they provide context, not certainty.

• **Lower ranges** often indicate higher perceived risk and typically result in higher costs, tighter terms, or additional conditions.

• **Middle ranges** reflect developing or moderate credit profiles where outcomes depend heavily on stability, utilization, and recent behavior.

• **Upper ranges** signal stronger credit profiles and tend to unlock better pricing, lower costs, and more flexibility.

What matters most is not where your score falls on a chart, but **how your Middle Credit Score® positions you relative to lender pricing tiers at the moment you apply**. A small movement within a range can materially change cost, while a large movement that occurs too late may not matter at all.

This is why strategy, timing, and consistency matter more than chasing a specific number. Credit scores are evaluated in ranges, but lending decisions are made in context.

Risk

Risk is the lens through which every credit decision is evaluated. It answers one core question: *How likely is this borrower to repay as agreed, without disruption?*

Late payments, high utilization, frequent account changes, excessive inquiries, and reporting inconsistencies all increase perceived risk. Stable balances, clean reporting, time, and predictable behavior reduce it. Credit decisions are not emotional—they are statistical. Once you understand risk, you stop reacting to credit outcomes and start managing them.

Core Credit Concepts: Referenced in Chapter(s)
Risk → Chapters 7, 10
Core Credit Concepts: Representative Client File Example(s)
Risk → Ch. 7, 10 → Examples 94, 96

Section 2: Credit Reports & Data

Account Status

Account status describes how an account is labeled on your credit report: current, late, charged-off, closed, paid, settled, or delinquent.
This label carries more weight than many consumers realize. An account marked "settled" may still signal risk differently than one marked "paid as agreed." Understanding status language helps you know which items truly matter and which ones are cosmetic.

Credit Reports & Data: Referenced in Chapter(s)
Account Status → Chapters 4, 5, 10
Credit Reports & Data: Representative Client File Example(s)
Account Status → Ch. 5, 10 → Examples 33, 37, 96

Alternative Tradelines

Alternative tradelines include non-traditional credit data such as rent, utilities, phone bills, or subscription services when reported through approved channels.
These do not replace traditional credit, but they can supplement thin or limited profiles. As the credit system evolves, alternative data is becoming more relevant. The borrowers who benefit most are those who understand **when and how** to use it, not those who assume it automatically helps.

Credit Reports & Data: Referenced in Chapter(s)
Alternative Tradelines → Chapters 5, 6
Credit Reports & Data: Representative Client File Example(s)
Alternative Tradelines → Ch. 6 → Examples 50, 93

Authorized User

An authorized user is someone added to another person's credit account. When used correctly, this can help build or strengthen a credit profile by inheriting the account's history. When misused, it can backfire, especially if the primary user carries high balances or pays late. Authorized user accounts are **tools, not shortcuts**. They work best when the underlying account is old, low-balance, and perfectly paid. Lenders can usually tell when authorized use is strategic rather than artificial.

Credit Reports & Data: Referenced in Chapter(s)
Authorized User → Chapters 6, 10
Credit Reports & Data: Representative Client File Example(s)
Authorized User → Ch. 6 → Examples 50, 92

Bureau Discrepancy

A bureau discrepancy occurs when the same account reports differently across Experian, Equifax, and TransUnion. This can involve balances, payment status, dates, or even whether the account appears at all.
Discrepancies are one of the most common reasons a Middle Credit Score® is lower than expected. One inaccurate bureau can quietly drag the middle score down and change pricing tiers without warning.

Credit Reports & Data: Referenced in Chapter(s)
Bureau Discrepancy → Chapters 5, 10
Credit Reports & Data: Representative Client File Example(s)
Bureau Discrepancy → Ch. 5 → Example 33

Credit Monitoring

Credit monitoring is the ongoing practice of monitoring your credit, not checking a score occasionally, but maintaining awareness of activity, trends, and accuracy.
Proper monitoring is proactive. It helps you catch errors early, detect fraud quickly, and prepare for major financial decisions without surprises. It's not about obsession; it is about control.

Credit Reports & Data: Referenced in Chapter(s)
Credit Monitoring → Chapters 4, 6, 13
Credit Reports & Data: Representative Client File Example(s)
Credit Monitoring → Ch. 6, 13 → Examples 91, 97

Date of Last Activity (DLA)

The Date of Last Activity is the most recent date associated with meaningful action on an account, such as a payment, charge, or update.
This date can affect reporting timelines, dispute strategy, and how long an item remains visible. Misreported DLAs are a standard error and can unfairly extend the life of negative items if not corrected.

Credit Reports & Data: Referenced in Chapter(s)
Date of Last Activity (DLA) → Chapters 4, 10
Credit Reports & Data: Representative Client File Example(s)
Date of Last Activity (DLA) → Ch. 10 → Example 96

Dispute

A dispute is the formal process of challenging inaccurate or incomplete information on your credit report. Disputes are not arguments; they are **documentation-driven corrections**.
When done correctly, disputes can remove outdated balances, incorrect late payments, duplicate accounts, or reporting errors that suppress your Middle Credit Score®. When done poorly—or excessively, they can delay underwriting, pause approvals, or create credibility concerns - precision, timing, and documentation matter.

Credit Reports & Data: Referenced in Chapter(s)
Dispute → Chapters 4, 5
Credit Reports & Data: Representative Client File Example(s)
Dispute → Ch. 5 → Examples 33, 37

Reporting Accuracy

Reporting accuracy means the information on your credit report matches reality: balances, dates, ownership, status, and payment history.
Inaccurate reporting doesn't just hurt scores; it erodes trust in your profile. Accurate data is the foundation of fair lending decisions. Without it, even good borrowers can be mispriced.

Credit Reports & Data: Referenced in Chapter(s)
Reporting Accuracy → Chapters 4, 5, 10
Credit Reports & Data: Representative Client File Example(s)
Reporting Accuracy → Ch. 5 → Examples 33, 37

Reporting Cycle

A reporting cycle is the period during which creditors send updated account information to credit bureaus, typically once per month. This timing matters more than most people realize. You can pay your card on time and still show high utilization if the balance is reported before the payment posts.
Understanding reporting cycles allows you to manage utilization intentionally instead of accidentally suppressing your score at the worst possible time.

Credit Reports & Data: Referenced in Chapter(s)
Reporting Cycle → Chapters 5, 6

Credit Reports & Data: Representative Client File Example(s)
Reporting Cycle → Ch. 6 → Examples 50, 93

Tradeline

A tradeline is any account that appears on your credit report, credit cards, auto loans, mortgages, student loans, collections, and more. Each tradeline tells a story: when it was opened, how it's been paid, how much is owed, and whether it's current or delinquent.

Lenders don't just count tradelines; they evaluate their **quality, age, and consistency**. A few well-managed tradelines over time often outperform a file filled with short-lived or erratic accounts. Strong tradelines build trust. Weak ones create doubt, even if the score looks acceptable.

Credit Reports & Data: Referenced in Chapter(s)
Tradeline → Chapters 4, 6, 10
Credit Reports & Data: Representative Client File Example(s)
Tradeline → Ch. 6, 10 → Examples 50, 96

Tri-Merge Report

A Tri-Merge credit report combines data from Experian, Equifax, and TransUnion into one side-by-side report. This is what most mortgage lenders use, and it's where inconsistencies become visible. One bureau may show an account as paid, another as late, and a third may not show it at all.

That's why Tri-Merge reports matter so much because your Middle Credit Score® is selected from this combined view. If one bureau is wrong, your outcome can change. This is often where borrowers lose money without realizing why, simply because they never saw the discrepancies the lender saw.

Credit Reports & Data: Referenced in Chapter(s)
Tri-Merge Report → Chapters 4, 5, 10
Credit Reports & Data: Representative Client File Example(s)
Tri-Merge Report → Ch. 5, 10 → Example 37

Section 3: Scoring & Pricing

Cost of Credit

The cost of credit is the **total financial impact** of borrowing, not just the monthly payment.
It includes interest, fees, mortgage insurance (PMI), opportunity cost, and long-term pricing differences. Credit decisions compound over time. A slight pricing difference today can translate into tens of thousands of dollars over the life of a loan. This is why understanding scoring and pricing is not optional; it is financial self-defense.

Scoring & Pricing: Referenced in Chapter(s)
Cost of Credit → Chapters 7, 10, 13
Scoring & Pricing: Representative Client File Example(s)
Cost of Credit → Ch. 7, 13 → Examples 96, 97

FICO® Model

A FICO® model is the mathematical system used to translate your credit behavior into a score. What most consumers don't realize is that there isn't just one FICO® score; there are multiple versions, and different lenders use different models.

Mortgage lenders often rely on older, more conservative FICO® models than credit card issuers. That's why the score you see online may not match the score used to price your loan. Understanding **which model is being used** matters more than chasing a single number because the model determines how your behavior is interpreted.

Scoring & Pricing: Referenced in Chapter(s)
FICO® Model → Chapters 4, 10
Scoring & Pricing: Representative Client File Example(s)
FICO® Model → Ch. 10 → Example 96

Interest Rate vs. APR

The interest rate reflects the cost of borrowing the principal amount. APR (Annual Percentage Rate) reflects the **actual cost of the loan**, including interest plus specific fees.
Two loans can have the same interest rate but very different APRs. That difference matters. APR tells you which loan is cheaper over time. Borrowers who focus only on the interest rate often miss where the real cost is hiding.

Scoring & Pricing: Referenced in Chapter(s)
Interest Rate vs. APR → Chapters 7, 10
Scoring & Pricing: Representative Client File Example(s)
Interest Rate vs. APR → Ch. 10 → Example 96

Loan Level Price Adjustments (LLPAs)

Loan Level Price Adjustments are costs applied to a loan based on risk factors such as credit score, loan-to-value (LTV), debt-to-income ratio (DTI), occupancy type, or property type.

LLPAs are common in mortgage lending and are often invisible to borrowers. They may appear as higher rates, higher fees, or both. Strong credit reduces LLPAs. Weaker credit increases them. This is one of the most direct ways in which credit quality affects long-term costs.

Scoring & Pricing: Referenced in Chapter(s)
LLPAs → Chapters 7, 10
Scoring & Pricing: Representative Client File Example(s)
LLPAs → Ch. 7, 10 → Examples 94, 96

Pricing Tier

A pricing tier is the category lenders use to determine interest rates, fees, and overall loan cost. These tiers are typically tied to score ranges, but they're influenced by the complete credit profile, not just the number.

Moving from one tier to the next doesn't require perfection. Sometimes a 10–20 point shift in the Middle Credit Score® can unlock dramatically better terms. This is where real money is made or lost—often without borrowers realizing it because pricing tiers quietly control long-term cost.

Scoring & Pricing: Referenced in Chapter(s)
Pricing Tier → Chapters 7, 10, 13
Scoring & Pricing: Representative Client File Example(s)
Pricing Tier → Ch. 7, 10, 13 → Examples 34, 96

Rate Sheet

A rate sheet is the internal pricing table lenders use to assign interest rates and costs based on score tiers, risk factors, and loan characteristics.

Borrowers never see the rate sheet, but it controls outcomes. Small changes in credit score, utilization, or risk factors can move a borrower from one line of the rate sheet to another, changing pricing dramatically without changing approval status.

Scoring & Pricing: Referenced in Chapter(s)
Rate Sheet → Chapters 7, 10
Scoring & Pricing: Representative Client File Example(s)
Rate Sheet → Ch. 10 → Example 96

Score Tier / Risk Tier

Score tiers, also called risk tiers, are the ranges lenders use to group borrowers by perceived risk. These tiers are not about approval versus denial; they are about **cost**. Two borrowers may both qualify, but the one in a lower tier will pay more in interest, fees, or adjustments. Understanding score tiers help borrowers stop asking, "Will I get approved?" and start asking, "What will this cost me?"

Scoring & Pricing: Referenced in Chapter(s)
Score Tier / Risk Tier → Chapters 7, 10
Scoring & Pricing: Representative Client File Example(s)
Score Tier / Risk Tier → Ch. 7, 10 → Examples 94, 96

Snapshot vs Trended Scoring

Snapshot scoring evaluates your credit at a single moment in time. Trended scoring evaluates how your behavior changes across months.

A snapshot might show low utilization today, but trended data reveals whether that's normal or temporary. As scoring models evolve, trend matters more. Lenders trust patterns more than one-time improvements.

Scoring & Pricing: Referenced in Chapter(s)
Snapshot vs. Trended Scoring → Chapters 6, 10
Scoring & Pricing: Representative Client File Example(s)
Snapshot vs. Trended Scoring → Ch. 6 → Example 50

Trended Data

Trended data looks at how your credit behavior changes over time, not just where it stands today. Instead of a snapshot, it shows a pattern.
Are balances rising month after month? Are they being paid down steadily? Are you consistently relying on credit or using it sparingly? Newer scoring models increasingly reward stable, disciplined patterns and penalize repeated high utilization. In this system, **consistency beats intensity** every time.

Scoring & Pricing: Referenced in Chapter(s)
Trended Data → Chapters 6, 10
Scoring & Pricing: Representative Client File Example(s)
Trended Data → Ch. 6 → Examples 50, 93

Section 4: Lending & Decision Language

Conditional Approval

A conditional approval means the lender is willing to move forward *if* specific requirements are met. These conditions usually involve documentation, clarification, or verification, not a rejection.

Many borrowers panic at conditions, but they're normal. The key is responsiveness and accuracy. The faster conditions are satisfied, the smoother the path to final approval.

Lending & Decision Language: Referenced in Chapter(s)
Conditional Approval → Chapters 7, 10
Lending & Decision Language: Representative Client File Example(s)
Conditional Approval → Ch. 10 → Example 96

Credit Overlay

A credit overlay is an additional rule a lender applies on top of basic lending guidelines. These overlays vary by lender and are often the reason one lender says "no" while another says "yes" to the same borrower.

Overlays are not credit failures; they are policy decisions. Understanding overlays helps borrowers shop intelligently rather than assume the system is unfair or broken.

Lending & Decision Language: Referenced in Chapter(s)
Credit Overlay → Chapters 7, 10
Lending & Decision Language: Representative Client File Example(s)
Credit Overlay → Ch. 7 → Example 94

Debt-to-Income (DTI)

The debt-to-income (DTI) ratio measures how much of your gross monthly income goes toward debt payments. It's calculated by dividing total monthly debt obligations by gross monthly income. Even with a strong Middle Credit Score®, a high DTI can limit approvals or raise costs. DTI answers a simple question lenders care deeply about: *Can this borrower comfortably handle the payment and life at the same time?* Lower DTI equals more flexibility, better options, and stronger positioning.

Lending & Decision Language: Referenced in Chapter(s)
DTI → Chapters 7, 10
Lending & Decision Language: Representative Client File Example(s)
DTI → Ch. 7, 10 → Examples 94, 96

Decision Score

The decision score is the specific credit score a lender uses to approve and price a loan. In mortgage lending, this is often the Middle Credit Score® derived from a Tri-Merge credit report using a specific FICO® model. This is the score that matters most in real-world outcomes. Many consumers focus on the highest score they see, but lenders price based on the decision score. Understanding which score drives the decision changes how you prepare—and how much you ultimately pay.

Lending & Decision Language: Referenced in Chapter(s)
Decision Score → Chapters 4, 10
Lending & Decision Language: Representative Client File

Example(s)
Decision Score → Ch. 10 → Example 96

Hard vs. Soft Inquiry

A soft inquiry occurs when credit is checked for informational purposes, such as monitoring or pre-qualification, and does not impact your score. A hard inquiry occurs when you apply for credit and can temporarily affect your score. One or two hard inquiries aren't harmful, but repeated or unnecessary inquiries, especially before a primary loan, can signal risk. Timing matters. Strategic borrowers safeguard their inquiries the same way they protect their utilization.

Lending & Decision Language: Referenced in Chapter(s)
Hard vs. Soft Inquiry → Chapters 6, 10
Lending & Decision Language: Representative Client File Example(s)
Hard vs. Soft Inquiry → Ch. 6 → Example 50

Loan-to-Value (LTV)

Loan-to-Value measures how much you're borrowing compared to the value of the property. A higher LTV means more lender risk. A lower LTV means more borrower equity. LTV is factored into pricing decisions alongside credit. Strong credit can offset higher LTV in some cases, while weaker credit combined with high LTV often increases rates, fees, or insurance costs. Lenders evaluate both together, not in isolation.

Lending & Decision Language: Referenced in Chapter(s)
LTV → Chapters 7, 10
Lending & Decision Language: Representative Client File

Example(s)
LTV → Ch. 7, 10 → Examples 94, 96

PMI (Private Mortgage Insurance)

Private Mortgage Insurance is typically required when a borrower puts less than 20% down on a conventional mortgage. PMI protects the lender, not the borrower, and the borrower's creditworthiness influences its cost.
A higher Middle Credit Score® can significantly reduce PMI costs, sometimes by hundreds of dollars per month. PMI is one of the clearest examples of how credit impacts affordability beyond interest rates alone.

Lending & Decision Language: Referenced in Chapter(s)
PMI → Chapters 7, 10
Lending & Decision Language: Representative Client File Example(s)
PMI → Ch. 7, 10 → Examples 94, 96

Pre-Qualification vs. Pre-Approval

Pre-qualification is an estimate based primarily on information you provide. It's informal and often based on soft data. Pre-approval is a verified review that includes documentation, credit checks, and lender validation.
Pre-qualification gives you a range. Pre-approval gives you leverage. Many consumers mistake pre-qualification for certainty, and that misunderstanding leads to disappointment later. If timing matters, pre-approval is where clarity begins.

Lending & Decision Language: Referenced in Chapter(s)
Pre-Qualification vs. Pre-Approval → Chapters 7, 10
Lending & Decision Language: Representative Client File

Example(s)
Pre-Qualification vs. Pre-Approval → Ch. 7 → Example 94

Underwriting

Underwriting is the process lenders use to evaluate risk before approving a loan. It's not personal; it is procedural. Underwriters review your income, assets, liabilities, credit history, and overall stability to determine whether lending to you makes financial sense under their guidelines. This is where credit stops being abstract and becomes actionable. Your Middle Credit Score®, utilization, payment history, and consistency all come into focus here. Strong underwriting outcomes come from preparation, not persuasion.

Lending & Decision Language: Referenced in Chapter(s)
Underwriting → Chapters 7, 10
Lending & Decision Language: Representative Client File Example(s)
Underwriting → Ch. 10 → Example 96

Section 5: Advanced Credit Signals

Account Churn

Account churn refers to **opening and closing accounts repeatedly** over a short time. Even if accounts are paid on time, frequent openings and closures create instability. Lenders prefer continuity. Long-standing accounts with responsible usage tell a stronger story than constantly "optimizing" or chasing new offers.

Advanced Credit Signals: Referenced in Chapter(s)
Account Churn → Chapters 6, 10

Advanced Credit Signals: Representative Client File Example(s)
Account Churn → Ch. 6 → Example 50

Balance Trending

Balance trending evaluates whether revolving balances are **rising, flat, or falling over time**. Even on-time payments don't offset upward balance trends. Rising balances signal growing pressure. Flat balances suggest stagnation. Declining balances, especially steadily, signal improving stability. This is one of the most powerful silent indicators in modern scoring and underwriting.

Advanced Credit Signals: Referenced in Chapter(s)
Balance Trending → Chapters 6, 10
Advanced Credit Signals: Representative Client File Example(s)
Balance Trending → Ch. 6 → Examples 50, 93

Behavior Consistency Window

This is the time period lenders review to confirm stability, often the **60 to 120 days before application**. What you do in this window matters more than what you did a year ago. Consistent behavior here reassures lenders that your current profile is intentional and sustainable.

Advanced Credit Signals: Referenced in Chapter(s)
Behavior Consistency Window → Chapters 6, 10
Advanced Credit Signals: Representative Client File Example(s)
Behavior Consistency Window → Ch. 6 → Examples 91, 93

Credit Mix Quality

Credit mix quality evaluates **how responsibly different types of credit are managed**; not just how many types exist. Having multiple account types doesn't help if they're poorly handled. A smaller mix managed cleanly is stronger than a complex mix managed inconsistently. Quality always beats quantity.

Advanced Credit Signals: Referenced in Chapter(s)
Credit Mix Quality → Chapters 6, 10
Advanced Credit Signals: Representative Client File Example(s)
Credit Mix Quality → Ch. 6 → Examples 50, 92

Credit Utilization Distribution

Credit utilization distribution looks at **how balances are spread across accounts**, not just the total utilization percentage.
A borrower with 20% total utilization can still look risky if one card is maxed out and the rest are unused. Lenders notice concentration. Balanced, evenly managed utilization signals control. Spikes on a single card, especially repeatedly, signal stress, even when the overall math looks fine.

Advanced Credit Signals: Referenced in Chapter(s)
Credit Utilization Distribution → Chapters 5, 6
Advanced Credit Signals: Representative Client File Example(s)
Credit Utilization Distribution → Ch. 6 → Examples 50, 93

Dormant vs Active Tradelines

This signal looks at whether accounts show **recent, responsible activity**. Dormant accounts don't hurt, but they don't help much either. Active accounts with low balances and on-time payments reinforce positive behavior. Lenders want to see that credit is being *used well*, not just existing.

Advanced Credit Signals: Referenced in Chapter(s)
Dormant vs. Active Tradelines → Chapters 6, 10
Advanced Credit Signals: Representative Client File Example(s)
Dormant vs. Active Tradelines → Ch. 6 → Example 92

File Thickness

File thickness describes how much usable data exists in a credit profile. A thin file may have a high score, but a limited history. A thick file shows behavior over time. Lenders trust depth. The more consistent data they can review, the more confident they are in pricing and approval decisions.

Advanced Credit Signals: Referenced in Chapter(s)
File Thickness → Chapters 6, 10
Advanced Credit Signals: Representative Client File Example(s)
File Thickness → Ch. 6 → Example 50

Inquiry Velocity

Inquiry velocity measures **how frequently credit inquiries occur within a short period**.

One inquiry isn't a concern. Several inquiries clustered together raise questions. High inquiry velocity suggests urgency, stress, or reactive borrowing. Lenders don't just count inquiries; they look at *timing and intent*.

Advanced Credit Signals: Referenced in Chapter(s)
Inquiry Velocity → Chapters 6, 10
Advanced Credit Signals: Representative Client File Example(s)
Inquiry Velocity → Ch. 6 → Example 50

Payment Hierarchy

Payment hierarchy reflects **which obligations a borrower prioritizes when money is tight**.
Mortgage, auto, and primary credit cards tell lenders more than secondary accounts. A borrower who protects core obligations even under pressure signal's reliability. Missed payments on key tradelines carry more weight than people realize.

Advanced Credit Signals: Referenced in Chapter(s)
Payment Hierarchy → Chapters 6, 10
Advanced Credit Signals: Representative Client File Example(s)
Payment Hierarchy → Ch. 6 → Example 91

Profile Intentionality

Profile intentionality answers a simple question: *Does this credit file look planned or reactive?* Intentional profiles show restraint, timing, and strategy. Reactive profiles show spikes, quick fixes, and last-minute moves. Lenders trust borrowers who appear to understand their own financial behavior.

Advanced Credit Signals: Referenced in Chapter(s)
Profile Intentionality → Chapters 6, 13
Advanced Credit Signals: Representative Client File Example(s)
Profile Intentionality → Ch. 6, 13 → Examples 91, 97

Revolving Dependency

Revolving dependency occurs when a borrower consistently relies on credit cards to support monthly cash flow. This isn't about using cards, it's about *needing* them. If balances stay high month after month and only minimum payments are made, the file suggests dependency rather than flexibility. Lenders prefer borrowers who *can* use credit, not borrowers who *must*.

Advanced Credit Signals: Referenced in Chapter(s)
Revolving Dependency → Chapters 6, 10
Advanced Credit Signals: Representative Client File Example(s)
Revolving Dependency → Ch. 6 → Examples 50, 92

Risk Layering

Risk layering occurs when **multiple moderate risks stack together**. A single risk may be acceptable. Several at once, high utilization, recent inquiries, high LTV, and thin reserves compound concern. Even if each risk is "within limits," the combination can affect pricing or approval strength.

Advanced Credit Signals: Referenced in Chapter(s)
Risk Layering → Chapters 7, 10

Advanced Credit Signals: Representative Client File Example(s)
Risk Layering → Ch. 7, 10 → Examples 94, 96

Section 6: Additional Useful Terms

Avalanche Method

The avalanche method is a debt repayment strategy that prioritizes paying off the highest-interest debt first while maintaining minimum payments on all other accounts. Mathematically, this approach saves the most money over time because it reduces interest faster. From a credit perspective, it can also improve utilization more efficiently when high-interest revolving accounts are involved. This method works best for disciplined borrowers who can stay focused on long-term savings rather than short-term emotional wins.

Additional Useful Terms: Referenced in Chapter(s)
Avalanche Method → Chapters 6, 13
Additional Useful Terms: Representative Client File Example(s)
Avalanche Method → Ch. 6, 13 → Examples 91, 97

Bankruptcy vs. Chapter 7

Bankruptcy is the legal process designed to provide relief when debts become unmanageable. Chapter 7 is a specific type of bankruptcy that typically involves the liquidation of non-exempt assets to discharge qualifying unsecured debts. From a credit standpoint, Chapter 7 has a severe short-term impact but can provide long-term recovery when paired with disciplined rebuilding. The key distinction borrowers often miss is this:

bankruptcy is not the end of credit, it's a reset point. What matters most is how credit behavior changes after discharge.

Additional Useful Terms: Referenced in Chapter(s)
Bankruptcy vs. Chapter 7 → Chapters 8, 13
Additional Useful Terms: Representative Client File Example(s)
Bankruptcy vs. Chapter 7 → Ch. 8, 13 → Examples 62, 91

Credit Monitoring Apps

Credit monitoring apps provide alerts when changes occur on your credit report, such as new accounts, inquiries, or balance updates. These tools are helpful for awareness, but they are not a strategy. Apps show activity; they don't explain lender impact, scoring models, or decision scores. Used correctly, they act as an early-warning system. Used incorrectly, they create false confidence. Monitoring should support intentional management, not replace it.

Additional Useful Terms: Referenced in Chapter(s)
Credit Monitoring Apps → Chapters 4, 6
Additional Useful Terms: Representative Client File Example(s)
Credit Monitoring Apps → Ch. 6 → Example 50

Credit Reporting Agencies (CRAs)

Credit reporting agencies are independent companies that collect, maintain, and distribute consumer credit data to lenders and other authorized parties. In the United States, the three primary credit reporting agencies are **Experian**, **Equifax**, and **TransUnion**.
Each agency maintains its own database. Creditors are not required to report to all three, nor are they required to report

information in the same way or at the same time. As a result, your credit reports can and often do differ across bureaus.

These differences matter because lenders frequently evaluate credit using data from all three bureaus. In mortgage lending, those reports are combined into a Tri-Merge report, and the Middle Credit Score® is selected from that combined view. One inaccurate or incomplete bureau can materially affect approval, pricing, or both often without the borrower realizing why.

Additional Useful Terms: Referenced in Chapter(s)
Credit Reporting Agencies (Credit Bureaus) → *Chapters 4, 5, 10, 13*
Additional Useful Terms: Representative Client File Example(s)
Credit Reporting Agencies (Credit Bureaus) →*Ch. 5,13*
→*Examples 33, 37, 92, 96*

Goodwill Request

A goodwill request is a written appeal to a creditor asking them to remove a late payment or negative mark as a courtesy after the account has been brought current. These requests are not disputes; they acknowledge the mistake while demonstrating a history of responsibility. Success depends on timing, documentation, and tone. While not guaranteed, goodwill requests can be effective when a borrower shows consistency before and after the issue. They are relationship-based, not rights-based.

Additional Useful Terms: Referenced in Chapter(s)
Goodwill Request → Chapters 4, 5
Additional Useful Terms: Representative Client File Example(s)
Goodwill Request → Ch. 5 → Example 37

Mid-Cycle Payments

Mid-cycle payments are payments made before a creditor reports the balance to the credit bureaus, often before the statement closing date. This strategy can lower reported utilization even if the account is used regularly. It's especially effective for borrowers who pay in full but still show high balances due to reporting timing. Mid-cycle payments don't change how much you owe—they change what gets reported. That distinction alone can protect pricing tiers and stabilize scores.

Additional Useful Terms: Referenced in Chapter(s)
Mid-Cycle Payments → Chapters 5, 6
Additional Useful Terms: Representative Client File Example(s)
Mid-Cycle Payments → Ch. 6 → Example 50

Negotiations

Negotiations involve direct communication with creditors or collection agencies to resolve outstanding debts under agreed terms. This may include payment plans, settlements, or pay-for-delete agreements when available. Effective negotiation is calm, documented, and intentional. Emotional or rushed negotiations often create worse outcomes. When done correctly negotiation is not about escaping responsibility; it's about resolving obligations in a way that minimizes long-term credit damage.

Additional Useful Terms: Referenced in Chapter(s)
Negotiations → *Chapters 5, 8, 10*

Additional Useful Terms: Representative Client File Example(s)
Negotiations → *Ch. 5, 8, 10* → *Examples 10, 12, 21, 23, 26, 30, 38, 39, 42, 50, 54, 71, 79, 82, 84*

Settlement Documentation

Settlement documentation is written proof that a debt has been resolved under agreed terms. This includes settlement letters, payment confirmations, and updated account status notices. Without documentation, a settlement is incomplete even if payment was made. Proper documentation protects against re-reporting errors, collection reactivation, or future disputes. In credit, if it isn't documented, it didn't happen.

Additional Useful Terms: Referenced in Chapter(s)
Settlement Documentation → *Chapters 5, 8, 10*
Additional Useful Terms: Representative Client File Example(s)
Settlement Documentation → *(No Client File Example)*

Final Credit Terms Note:

This section works best as a **practical companion** to the earlier chapters' terms borrowers often encounter during cleanup, recovery, or optimization. These aren't abstract definitions. They are tools that show up when real decisions are being made.

CLOSING REMARKS

If you have made it to this final page, take a moment to acknowledge what you've done. You did not just read a book; you invested in your financial future. You took the time to understand something that impacts nearly every major decision you will make in life, yet is rarely explained clearly or honestly. That alone puts you ahead of where you were when you started.

When most people first hear the term "Middle Credit Score®," it feels abstract, just another financial phrase buried in fine print. But now you know better. You understand that your Middle Credit Score is not just a number; it is a reflection of habits, consistency, and decision-making over time. More importantly, you understand that it is something you can influence.

Over the years, I have watched people transform their financial lives, not by doing anything extreme, but by doing the right things consistently. Paying attention, asking better questions, and making informed choices. This book was designed to give you that same advantage. The strategies you've learned here are not short-term fixes; they are a framework you can use for the rest of your life.

Your credit journey does not end here. It evolves. New goals will appear. Life will change. Markets will shift. But the foundation you have built, understanding how credit really works, how to protect your Middle Credit Score, and how to align it with your long-term plans, will travel with you through every stage.

CLOSING REMARKS

I encourage you to treat what you have learned as a living system. Track your progress. Reflect often. Use a journal. Adjust when needed. Celebrate improvements, no matter how small, and when challenges arise, you will return to the principles in this book. They were built to withstand real life, not ideal circumstances.

Finally, do not keep this knowledge to yourself. Share it. Teach it. Talk about it with your family, your children, your friends. Financial literacy is one of the few things that multiplies when it's shared. If this book helps you make better decisions, and those decisions help someone else, the impact goes far beyond numbers on a credit report. Your Middle Credit Score® is no longer something that happens to you. It is something you understand. Something you manage. Something you use, and with that, you're no longer guessing you're moving forward with intention.

That is how real financial empowerment begins.

I want to end this book by being very clear about why it exists.

I did not write this because I wanted to publish a book. I wrote it because after decades in real estate, lending, and credit work, I realized something uncomfortable: **too many people are paying for mistakes they were never taught how to avoid.**

I have sat across the table from thousands of smart, hardworking people who lacked neither discipline nor ambition. What they lacked was clarity. No one ever explained how credit really works. No one explained why the Middle Credit Score matters more than the number they see on a credit scoring app or website. No one explained how one decision at 25 can quietly cost them tens of thousands of dollars by 45. And by the time they found out, the damage was already done.

I wish a book like this had existed earlier in my career, not for my clients, but for me.

I learned most of what is in these pages the hard way: through files, denials, approvals, disputes, rebuilds, and real consequences. I watched patterns repeat across different income levels, cities, and life stages. Over time, it became impossible to ignore one truth: **credit is not confusing; it is simply poorly explained.**

This book is my attempt to fix that.

Not by simplifying the truth.
Not by promising shortcuts.
And not by telling you what you "should" do.

But by giving you the same clarity I provide the people I work with one-on-one, the clarity that turns anxiety into confidence, and confusion into control.

With that clarity comes responsibility.

In this book, I have included 97 client stories that represent years of honest conversations, real consequences, and real progress. Each one reinforces why understanding your Middle Credit Score® changes outcomes.

Once you understand how your credit works, you cannot unknow it. You stop blaming the system. You stop guessing. You start making decisions with intention. That responsibility is not a burden; it is freedom. Because when you understand the rules, you can play the game on your terms.

If this book helped you see your finances differently, use it. Revisit it. Share it. Teach someone else what you've learned. That is how change compounds, not just through better scores, but through better habits, better decisions, and better outcomes over time.

I do not measure this book's success by how many pages you read straight through.
I measure it by whether, six months from now, you are

calmer, more prepared, and more confident when life asks you to make a financial decision.

If that happens even once, then writing this book was worth it.

Glenn Clark
Founder, Middle Credit Score®

ACKNOWLEDGEMENTS

This book exists because of people who stood with me long before the idea of writing it ever felt possible. While *What Is Your Middle Credit Score?* is rooted in nearly three decades of experience in real estate, lending, and consumer credit, it is also the result of encouragement, belief, accountability, and support that came from those closest to me.

First, my family. Everything I understand about resilience, responsibility, and perseverance started there. To my mother and father, thank you for instilling discipline, work ethic, and the expectation that I carry myself with integrity, even when no one is watching. To my stepfather, thank you for your strength, consistency, and presence when it mattered most. To my sisters, brothers, and nephews, you remind me why financial education matters beyond theory. Credit decisions do not just affect individuals; they affect families, futures, and generations. This book was written with that understanding.

To my wife, **Olga**, your belief in me never wavered, even during the moments when mine did. You understood the weight of this book before most people ever saw it. You saw the late nights, the rewrites, the pressure to get it right, not just for business, but for impact. Your patience, strength, and steady encouragement made this possible. And to my daughters, **Mayima and Zoe**, you are the reason this work matters. Every lesson in this book, every framework, every example exists so your future, and the futures of kids like you, can be built on knowledge instead of confusion. I want you to grow up understanding money, credit, and responsibility without fear.

To my close friends: **Jorge, Dwayne, Rashid, Paul, Arthur, Mouad, Michael, Shajib, Chris, Eric, Jose, and Joe**, thank you for being the people who checked in, listened, challenged me, and reminded me who I am when the work felt heavy. You did not just support the idea of this book; you supported the person writing it. That matters more than you know.

To the professionals and mentors who shaped my career: **Steve D., Anna G., and Frank B.**: thank you for the standards you set and the lessons you taught, often without realizing it. You showed me how systems work, how decisions are made, and how small details can carry massive consequences. Many of the insights in this book are built on foundations I learned while working alongside you.

To my professors: **Jason, Dr. Eaton, Dr. Neck, and Dr. Waddell**, thank you for sharpening how I think, not just what I know. You taught me how to analyze systems, question assumptions, and connect theory to real-world outcomes. That mindset is woven throughout this book, especially in how I approach credit not as a number, but as a behavioral system.

Finally, to every client I have worked with over the years, thank you for trusting me with your stories, your struggles, and your goals. The "From My Client Files" examples

ACKNOWLEDGEMENTS

throughout this book exist because real people were willing to learn, adjust, and take control of their financial lives. Your experiences are the proof that understanding credit, especially the Middle Credit Score®, can change outcomes when applied with intention and consistency.

I wrote this book because I wish it existed earlier in my career. I watched too many good people pay more than they should have, not because they were irresponsible, but because they were never taught how the system works. If this book helps even one reader replace confusion with clarity, fear with control, and guesswork with strategy, then the work was worth it.

Thank you to everyone who helped me carry this from idea to reality. This book is stronger because of you.

Glenn Clark

ABOUT THE AUTHOR

Glenn Clark is a real estate broker, former co-owner of a mortgage company, and credit strategist with nearly three decades of experience in lending, credit, and consumer decision-making. Over the course of his career, he has reviewed thousands of credit files, structured countless mortgage transactions, and helped consumers navigate some of the most important financial decisions of their lives.

Before writing *What Is Your Middle Credit Score?* Glenn spent years inside the lending system itself. He served as a top-producing loan officer, managed teams, and co-owned a mortgage company, giving him firsthand insight into how credit is evaluated behind the scenes. He didn't just see approvals and denials; he saw pricing tiers, underwriting notes, risk assessments, and the real reasons borrowers paid more—or less—for the same opportunities. That exposure revealed a persistent problem: consumers were being judged by a system they were never taught to understand.

Throughout his career, Glenn repeatedly watched capable, responsible people get mispriced, delayed, or denied, not because they were high risk, but because they misunderstood how credit decisions are made. The most common blind spot was the Middle Credit Score®, the score lenders often rely on for pricing and approval, yet almost no one explained it clearly. This book was written to close that gap.

Glenn is the founder of Middle Credit Score® and Browse Lenders®, platforms designed to educate consumers and increase transparency between borrowers and lenders. His work focuses on replacing confusion with clarity, fear with structure, and reactive financial behavior with intentional strategy. Rather than promoting shortcuts or "credit hacks," Glenn teaches habits, systems, and decision frameworks that hold up in real life during job changes, market shifts, medical events, and significant milestones like homeownership.

At the core of Glenn's philosophy is a simple belief: credit is not a judgment of character; it is a record of behavior. When people understand what the system measures, they stop fearing it and start managing it. That shift does not just improve scores; it lowers long-term costs, expands options, and restores confidence. This book reflects the same approach Glenn has used with clients for years: practical, direct, and grounded in reality.

Outside of his professional work, Glenn is a husband, a father, and a lifelong student of personal growth and financial literacy. He believes that understanding credit is not just about individual success, but about creating stability that can be passed forward to families, communities, and future generations. *What Is Your Middle Credit Score?* was written not as a theory, but as a tool that readers can return to throughout different stages of life as their goals evolve.

www.ingramcontent.com/pod-product-compliance
Lightning Source LLC
Chambersburg PA
CBHW051342280526
45784CB00007B/2784